WALKING
LAKE GARDA AND ISEO

About the Author

Gillian Price was born in England but moved to Australia when young. After taking a degree in anthropology and working in adult education, she set off to travel through Asia and trek the Himalayas. The culmination of her journey was Venice where, her enthusiasm fired for mountains, the next logical step was towards the Dolomites, only hours away. Starting there, Gillian is steadily exploring the mountain ranges and flatter bits of Italy and bringing them to life for visitors in a series of outstanding guides for Cicerone.

When not out walking with Nicola, her Venetian cartographer husband, Gillian works as a freelance travel writer (www.gillianprice.eu). An adamant promoter of public transport to minimise impact in alpine areas, Gillian is also an active member of the Italian Alpine Club CAI and Mountain Wilderness.

Other Cicerone guides by the author

Across the Eastern Alps – the E5
Alpine Flowers
Gran Paradiso: Alta Via 2
Italy's Sibillini National Park
Shorter Walks in the Dolomites
The Tour of the Bernina
Through the Italian Alps – the GTA
Trekking in the Apennines
Trekking in the Dolomites
Walking and Trekking on Corfu
Walking in Italy's Stelvio
    National Park

Walking in Sicily
Walking in the Central Italian Alps
Walking in the Dolomites
Walking in Tuscany
Walking in Umbria
Walking Lake Como and Maggiore
Walking on Corsica
Walking on the Amalfi Coast
Walks and Treks in the
    Maritime Alps

WALKING
LAKE GARDA AND ISEO

by Gillian Price

JUNIPER HOUSE, MURLEY MOSS,
OXENHOLME ROAD, KENDAL, CUMBRIA LA9 7RL
www.cicerone.co.uk

© Gillian Price 2019
First edition 2019
ISBN: 978 1 78631 024 8

Printed in China on behalf of Latitude Press.
A catalogue record for this book is available from the British Library.

Maps by Nicola Regine.
All photographs are by the author unless otherwise stated.

To dear Nicola, my special sherpa

Acknowledgements

Firstly a great big 'thank you' to Jonathan Williams of Cicerone for suggesting we explore these breathtaking lakes! We had no idea they were so beautiful.

I'd like to acknowledge helpful suggestions from Roberto Ricca of Bresciatourism as well as the enthusiastic Tourist Office staff of Iseo, Limone, Riva del Garda, Torre del Benaco and Malcesine.

Updates to this Guide

While every effort is made by our authors to ensure the accuracy of guidebooks as they go to print, changes can occur during the lifetime of an edition. Any updates that we know of for this guide will be on the Cicerone website (www.cicerone.co.uk/1024/updatess), so please check before planning your trip. We also advise that you check information about such things as transport, accommodation and shops locally. Even rights of way can be altered over time. We are always grateful for information about any discrepancies between a guidebook and the facts on the ground, sent by email to updates@cicerone.co.uk or by post to Cicerone, Juniper House, Murley Moss, Oxenholme Road, Kendal LA9 7RL.

Register your book: To sign up to receive free updates, special offers and GPX files where available, register your book at www.cicerone.co.uk.

Front cover: The superb view over Lake Garda from the belvedere on Colmo di Malcesine, Monte Baldo (Walk 11)

CONTENTS

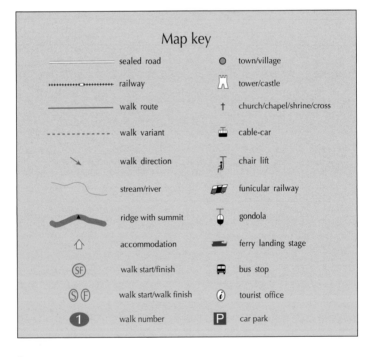

Map key

——————— sealed road	◎	town/village
+++++++○+++++++ railway	🏰	tower/castle
——————— walk route	†	church/chapel/shrine/cross
- - - - - - - - - walk variant	🚠	cable-car
↘ walk direction	🚡	chair lift
〜〜〜 stream/river	🚟	funicular railway
▬▲▬ ridge with summit	🚟	gondola
⇧ accommodation	⛴	ferry landing stage
⑤Ⓕ walk start/finish	🚌	bus stop
Ⓢ Ⓕ walk start/walk finish	ⓘ	tourist office
① walk number	🅿	car park

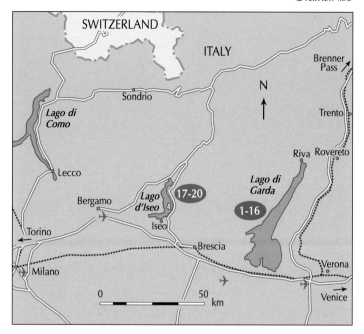

Mountain warning

Every mountain walk has its dangers, and those described in this guidebook are no exception. All who walk or climb in the mountains should recognise this and take responsibility for themselves and their companions along the way. The author and publisher have made every effort to ensure that the information contained in this guide was correct when it went to press, but, except for any liability that cannot be excluded by law, they cannot accept responsibility for any loss, injury or inconvenience sustained by any person using this book.

To call out the Mountain Rescue, ring 118: this will connect you via any available network. Once connected to the operator, ask for *Soccorso Alpino*.

The old Strada del Ponale along the northeastern edge of Lago di Garda (Walk 7)

INTRODUCTION

At the foot of the Alps in north Italy, the magnificent expanse of Lago di Garda is an irresistible magnet for sport and nature lovers, along with its attractive western neighbour, lesser known Lago d'Iseo. Only steps beyond the beautiful lakefronts and its promenades is a wonderful world of footpaths traversing woods and rugged mountain valleys, often making use of a network of age-old paved mule tracks linking remote hamlets. This guide describes a selection of 20 routes suitable for enthusiasts of all levels of experience and ability, from a leisurely waterfront stroll to a demanding extended hike to alpine heights. Well-marked straightforward routes can be enjoyed on walks that easily fit into the space of a day. And what's more, every single one can be accessed by the excellent local public transport network, be that ferry, train, bus, cable car or chair lift.

The two lakes are quite distinct in flavour and atmosphere – and both breathtakingly beautiful. How to decide which one to start with? In brief, Garda is more dramatic, vast and alpine in flavour, the upper lake hemmed in by awesome cliffs, while little brother Iseo is smaller, more remote, less touristy yet simply delightful. More details are given

Olives flourish in the warm climate

in the individual lake chapters. On the other hand further west are the great lakes of Como and Maggiore, described in a separate Cicerone guide *Walking Lake Como and Maggiore*. Rest assured that once your enthusiasm is fired you'll want to see all four!

Italy's great northern lakes were formed by ancient glaciers that spread down from the Alps towards the plains. When temperatures started to rise – around 12,000 years ago – the ice began to melt and retreat, leaving elongated troughs scooped out by the passage of the frozen mass. These gradually filled up with water, giving rise to the spectacular lakes seen today. Lying on a north–south axis, they resemble deep fjords, wedged between line after breathtaking line of rugged mountain ridges rising well over 2000m. Fed by rivers and streams running straight off the Alps, their crystal-clear waters reach a comfortable 24°C in midsummer.

PLANTS AND FLOWERS

These lakes are a delight for plant and flower lovers as the warm climate and altitude range guarantee both Mediterranean and alpine species. Wildflowers can be expected to start blooming at low altitudes in springtime as early as April and May, and from June through to August on the higher mountain ridges. Highlights include the gorgeous peonies in the 'Botanical Garden of Europe'

– namely Monte Baldo on Lago di Garda – as well as brilliant orange lilies in meadows, the concentrated blue-purple hue of the willow-leaved gentian that blooms in gay clumps on open grassland. Orchids are always a delight, and one special treasure is the rare insect orchid named after Lago di Garda (though not exclusive to that area): *Ophrys Benacensis*. An attractive and commonly encountered flowering bush is the smoke tree, its fluffy orange blooms reminiscent of clouds of smoke. Flower enthusiasts will appreciate the Cicerone mini guide *Alpine Flowers*.

High stone walls often boast magnificent bouquets of straggling caper plants, their open white petals brandishing purple pistils. It is their buds, picked and pickled or salted, which are the familiar ingredients of Italian cuisine. Moreover grape vines flourish in the mild climate as do olives, especially along the sun-blessed lake shores of Lago di Garda.

WILDLIFE

The hilly and mountainous surrounds of the lakes are home to a superb range of birds of prey such as kites and eagles that are easily spotted soaring overhead looking out for a meal, while myriad timid songbirds provide sonorous entertainment from the safety of tree cover.

Walkers in woods will often notice hoof marks in the mud and scratchings and diggings in the

(Clockwise from top left) Brilliant orange lily; delicate caper blooms; willow-leaved gentians; peonies on Monte Baldo

undergrowth, a sure sign of the presence of wild boar. Actual sightings are extremely rare as the creatures are very timid. Chances are better of spotting roe deer flitting between trees, while higher rocky terrain is home to the dainty goat-like chamois, recognisable for their trademark crochet-hook horns and dark patched rear quarters. Grassland over the 800m mark is home to colonies of endearing alpine marmots, often seen dashing across the meadows on a quest for sugary wildflowers to feast on.

GETTING THERE

Both lakes can easily be accessed by overseas visitors. Specific details for getting around them are given in the introduction to each chapter.

By air

For Lago di Garda, the airports at Brescia (www.aeroportobrescia.it) or Verona (www.aeroportoverona.it) are convenient whereas Bergamo's Orio Al Serio airport (www.sacbo.it) is handy for Lago d'Iseo as are Milan's Linate and Malpensa airports (www.sea-aeroportimilano.it).

The ferry landing stage at Iseo on Lago d'Iseo

ISEO
Partenze per MONTEISOLA ed altre destinazioni

By train

The international train line between Austria and Italy (Innsbruck–Verona) comes in handy for Lago di Garda with a handy stop at Rovereto, which has good bus links for Riva del Garda (Austrian rail www.oebb.at, Italian trains www.trenitalia.com).

LOCAL TRANSPORT

The extensive network of trains, buses, ferries and cable cars around and across Lago di Garda and Lago d'Iseo is both easy to use and unfailingly reliable. All the walks in this guidebook start and finish at public transport (and the book was researched by public transport). Local bus drivers know the roads and conditions like the back of their hand, leaving passengers free to sit back and enjoy the views. So visitors never need to think of hiring or taking their own car and so can avoid contributing to air pollution and traffic congestion in these magical places.

Generally speaking bus schedules follow the Italian school year, with extra runs during term time. Slightly reduced summer timetables correspond to the holidays, which fall around mid-June through to mid-September. Full ferry services are timetabled from March/April through to October/November; during winter services are cut back drastically, and some suspended. Exact dates vary from year to year, company to company and region to region, and can be checked on the websites listed under the individual lakes.

Reasonable pricing prevails everywhere: for instance, at the time of writing the ferry from Riva to Limone on Lago di Garda cost €5, and from Iseo to Peschiera on Monteisola

€3. Over 65ers are entitled to reductions. Day tickets are available – ask for *biglietto di libera circolazione* on Garda or *io viaggio* covering all public transport in Lombardia. The cable cars tend to be more expensive: the double-section Malcesine cable car on Lago di Garda costs €15 single, or €22 for the return trip.

Bus tickets should usually be purchased before a journey, either at the bus station or newsstands or tobacconists displaying the appropriate logo for the relevant transport company, then stamped on board. For trains, always remember to validate (stamp) tickets before boarding, so as to avoid a fine.

Specific details for buses, trains, ferries, cable cars and taxis are given at the beginning of each chapter.

INFORMATION

The Italian Tourist Board (www.enit.it) has offices all over the world and can help those planning to visit the Italian lakes with general information.

Information on accommodation, transport and what to see can be

USEFUL EXPRESSIONS

These expressions may come in useful when purchasing tickets.

One ticket/two tickets to Monteisola, please.	*Un biglietto/due biglietti per Monteisola, per favore.*
single	*andata/corsa semplice*
return	*andata e ritorno*
How much is that?	*Quanto costa?*
platform	*binario*
timetable	*orario*
Thank you	*Grazie*
You're welcome	*Prego*

The following words may be helpful for understanding timetables.

Cambio a.../coincidenza	Change at.../connection
estivo/invernale	summer/winter
feriale	working days (Monday to Saturday)
festivo	holidays (Sundays and public holidays)
giornaliero	daily
lunedì a venerdì/sabato	Monday to Friday/Saturday
navetta	shuttle service
sciopero	strike
scolastico	during school term

obtained from local tourist information offices and websites.

Lago di Garda
www.visitgarda.com

- Desenzano Tel 030 3748726
  www.provincia.brescia.it/turismo
- Gargnano Tel 0365 791243
  www.gargnanosulgarda.it
- Limone Tel 0365 918987
  www.visitlimonesulgarda.com
- Malcesine Tel 045 7400044
  www.visitmalcesine.com
- Peschiera sul Garda Tel 045 7550810
  www.tourismpeschiera.it
- Riva del Garda Tel 0464 554444
  www.gardatrentino.it
- San Zeno di Montagna
  Tel 045 6289296
  www.comunesanzenodi
  montagna.it
- Torbole Tel 0464 505177
  www.gardatrentino.it
- Torri di Benaco
  Tel 045 7225120
  www.tourism.verona.it
- Toscolano-Maderno
  Tel 0365 644298
  www.prolocotoscolanomaderno.
  com

Lago d'Iseo

- Iseo Tel 030 3748733
  www.visitlakeiseo.info
- Lovere Tel 035 962178
  www.visitlakeiseo.info
- Peschiera Maraglio, Monteisola
  Tel 030 9825088
  www.visitmonteisola.it

The lakes are renowned for their mild climate. Temperatures range from around 13°C in December to the high 20s in July.

Generally speaking the months of March through to June, spring to early summer, are perfect and highly recommended for walking as temperatures are comfortable, the vegetation is a brilliant green and the flowers blooming. However, September and October are wonderful as well, with marginally fewer visitors and clear crisp conditions once summer haze has dissipated. Midsummer (July and August) can get quite hot – up to 30°C – although an afternoon breeze is nearly always guaranteed. Of course the heat can be tempered by a dip in a lake (or your hotel swimming pool) or better still, a walk in a high place.

The high-altitude walking routes are usually out of bounds throughout the winter months due to snowfalls. However, crisp sunny winter days can make for perfect low-altitude walking with brilliant visibility. Be aware that ferry services are reduced from November through to March, when much accommodation closes, as do villas and gardens.

The lakes can get very busy on the main Italian public holidays: 1 January (New Year), 6 January (Epiphany), Easter Sunday and Monday, 25 April (Liberation Day), 1 May (Labour Day), 2 June (Republic Day), 15 August (Ferragosto), 1 November (All

Saints), 8 December (Immaculate Conception), 25-26 December (Christmas and Boxing Day).

ACCOMMODATION

The two lakes have a marvellous range of reasonably priced accommodation in hotels, B&Bs and campsites, as well as hostels and mountain huts. Suggestions for options in the middle price range (around €80–100 for a double room with breakfast) are given in the introductions to each lake; most have websites and accept credit card payments. A deposit may be required. Book well in advance around the Italian public holidays (see above) and the peak months of May and September. For self-catering possibilities contact the Tourist Offices or internet. All the major towns and villages have grocery stores and supermarkets, not to mention ATMs.

Remember that many places – but by no means all – close over the winter, usually from October/November to March/April, so check beforehand if planning on a low-season visit.

An overnight stay in a *rifugio* is always a memorable experience. These chalets – set on mountain slopes far from roads and villages, and accessible on foot – are staffed during the summer months and provide reasonably priced meals and dormitory accommodation for walkers and climbers. Contact details are given in the relevant walk descriptions (14 and 15).

If phoning from overseas to book accommodation preface the phone numbers with +39, country code for Italy, and always include the initial 0 of the area code, now incorporated into all Italian phone numbers. If calling from within Italy, dial that 0 as well. The only exceptions are Italian mobile phones which begin with 3, emergency numbers such as 118 for medical matters, or toll-free information services which start with 800.

FOOD AND DRINK

Foodies have to plenty to look forward to. The two lakes featured in this guide belong to the northern Italian regions of Lombardia, Trentino-Alto Adige and the Veneto, and each proudly nurtures its own gastronomic specialities. Some explanatory notes are given here to guide visitors, but generally speaking the best rule is to be adventurous and ask for the day's speciality, which will usually feature seasonal, locally sourced products. *Che cosa avete oggi?* means 'What's on today?'

In terms of dinner, Lombardia spells risotto heaven. Impossible to beat is *risotto alla milanese*, creamy rice cooked in a delicate meat broth, fragrant with saffron and often twinned with *ossobuco*, tender braised veal shank. Pasta comes in all sorts of wonderful shapes and mouth watering sauces. Unusual choices include *strangolapreti* ('priest stranglers'!), a Trentino dish of small gnocchi dumplings of spinach and potato

Many grape varieties flourish on sunny slopes around the lakes

drizzled with melted butter. On Lago di Garda *tagliolini con crema di limone* are thin ribbons of fresh pasta in a tangy lemon sauce.

In Lombardia on the weekend country restaurants do *Spiedo*: a selection of meat chunks liberally seasoned with fresh herbs such as sage, gently spit roasted and served with potatoes or *polenta* (cornmeal). Traditionally it also meant *uccellini*, birds hunted in the hills over the autumn months, but no longer.

Freshwater fish from the lakes features prominently on menus. The most common is *coregone* – also known as *lavarello* – which translates as whitefish. Its pale flesh, delicate and soft, is perfectly suited to a quick grilling or frying. There's also *alborella* which translates curiously as bleak, often dried and salted or served lightly fried.

Wine lists offer a kaleidoscope of flavours and experiences. In the southern reaches of Lago di Garda, in the Veneto, quaffable reds are copious, starting with Bardolino and Valpolicella that need little introduction, and moving on to more substantial – and stronger in both alcohol and taste – garnet-coloured Recioto and the legendary Amarone, whose price tag suggests it be reserved for a very special occasion.

One excellent dessert or snack is the Trentino speciality *torta sbrisolona*, a delicious type of crumbly shortbread made with chopped almonds.

Breakfast in Italy tends to be simple. Most Italians take a coffee as *cappuccino* (with frothy milk) or *espresso* (a strong, black concentrated shot), usually accompanied by a croissant, while standing at the local café. These days most middle-range hotels and B&Bs do a decent buffet breakfast with fruit, cereals, eggs, bread and a choice of hot beverage.

For picnic lunches, neighbourhood grocery shops (*alimentari*) or small supermarkets are usually happy to make up a fresh bread roll (*panino*) with your choice of filling. Any of the renowned Italian cured meats, such as fragrant *prosciutto crudo*, are perfect. Cheeses crafted from cow (*mucca*), sheep (*pecora*) or goat (*capra*) milk come in a huge range: soft, smooth, crumbly, tangy (and downright mouldy and stinky at times), as the mouth-watering display at any delicatessen can attest.

A note on drinking water: Italian domestic tap water (*acqua da rubinetto*) is always safe for drinking (*potabile* means drinkable), and by law is meticulously tested on a frequent basis. You can request it in any restaurant and café instead of bottled mineral water, which needs to be transported at a high cost to the environment. Thankfully there is a growing movement of people aware of and working to avoid such waste. For instance the innovative administrators of the Province of Brescia – from the eastern shore of Lago d'Iseo to the western edge of Lago di Garda – have installed dispensers of free water in towns and villages across their territory; filtered mains water, it comes chilled, fizzy or flat. This is a reinvention of the age-old tradition of the village fountain, still alive and commonplace in the majority of the alpine villages and hamlets visited during these walks.

WHAT TO TAKE

- Sun protection: hat, high-factor cream and sunglasses
- Bottle for drinking water
- Small daypack: shoulder and hand-held bags are unwise, as it's safer to have hands and arms free while walking
- Lightweight trekking boots, or decent pair of trainers or sports shoes, with good grip and thickish soles to protect your feet from loose stones; sandals are quite unsuitable
- Trekking poles for the high mountain routes
- Waterproof gear including lightweight jacket, rucksack cover, and optional overtrousers
- T-shirts and shorts during spring/ summer, layered with a light sweater or shirt for cooler conditions

Walking shoes with a good grip are essential, as seen on the scenic path to Cima delle Pozzette (Walk 12)

- Autum/winter visitors should pack warm clothes: long trousers, fleece or pullover, hat and gloves
- Basic first-aid kit
- Whistle, headlamp or torch, to be used if calling for help in an emergency
- Maps (see below) and compass

MAPS

Sketch maps are provided for each walk in this guidebook. In many cases these are sufficient for the walk, in combination with the walk description. However it is always a good idea to get hold of larger maps of the area for a number of reasons: they put places in a wider context, help you identify points of interest, plot your own routes and last but not least, are an essential tool for orientation if you lose your way. A good range of walking maps is available for the lakes, and information concerning specific maps is given in the introduction to each chapter. Some maps are available overseas at outdoor stores and bookshops, several can be downloaded from websites, while others are sold locally at the lakes.

DOS AND DON'TS

- Don't set out late in the day, even on a short walk. Always allow extra time for detours and wrong turns.
- Do find time to get in decent shape before setting out on your holiday, as it will maximise enjoyment. The wonderful scenery will be better appreciated when you're not in a state of exhaustion, and healthy walkers react better in an emergency.
- Don't walk on your own. Stick with your companions and don't lose sight of them; remember that the progress of the group should match that of the slowest member.
- Don't be overly ambitious; choose routes suited to your ability (and to that of the group). Read the walk description carefully before setting out.
- Avoid walking in brand new footwear, to reduce the likelihood of blisters; leave those old worn-out shoes at home, as they may be unsafe on slippery terrain. Choose your footwear carefully; comfort is essential.
- Check the weather forecast locally if possible and don't start out even on a short route if storms are forecast: paths can get slippery and mountainsides are prone to rockfalls.
- Carry weatherproof gear at all times, along with food and plenty of drinking water
- In electrical storms, don't shelter under trees or rock overhangs and keep away from metallic fixtures
- **Do not** rely on your mobile phone in an emergency as there is often no signal in the mountainous areas

- Carry any rubbish back to the village where it can be disposed of correctly. Even organic waste such as apple cores and orange peel is best not left lying around as it can upset the diet of animals and birds and irritate other visitors.
- Be considerate if you have to make a toilet stop. Carry a supply of small 'doggy bags' to deal with paper and tissues.
- Lastly, don't leave your common sense at home

EMERGENCIES

For medical matters, EU residents need a European Health Insurance Card (EHIC). Holders are entitled to free or subsidised emergency treatment in Italy, which has an excellent national health service. UK residents can apply online at www. dh.gov.uk. Australia has a similar reciprocal agreement – see www. humanservices.gov.au. Other nationalities should take out suitable equivalent insurance.

Travel insurance for a walking holiday is also strongly recommended, as the costs of rescue and repatriation can be considerable. Membership of the Italian Alpine Club www.cai.it is open to everyone and includes insurance for mountain rescue operations all over Europe.

- General emergency Tel 112
- *Polizia* (police) Tel 113
- Health-related emergencies including ambulance (*ambulanza*) and mountain rescue (*soccorso alpino*) Tel 118
- 'Help!' in Italian is *Aiuto!*, pronounced 'eye-you-tow'. *Pericolo* is 'danger'.

Should help be needed during a walk, use the following internationally recognised rescue signals: **six** signals per minute either visual (waving a handkerchief or flashing a torch) or audible (shouting or whistling), repeated after a pause of one minute. The answer is **three** visual or audible signals per minute, to be repeated after a one-minute pause. Anyone who sees or hears a call for assistance must contact the nearest source of help, a mountain hut or police station for example, as quickly as possible.

These hand signals (below) could be useful for communicating at a distance or with a helicopter.

Help required
Raise both arms above head to form a 'Y'

Help not required
Raise one arm above head and extend the other downward, to form the diagonal of an 'N'

USING THIS GUIDE

This is a selection of 20 day walks around Lago di Garda and Lago d'Iseo. (Another Cicerone guide-book covers *Walking Lake Como and Maggiore*). The aim was to describe the top routes without making the book too cumbersome and encyclo-paedic. Visitors wishing to do more of the multitudinous routes can enquire at the local Tourist Offices.

Most of the routes are waymarked with official CAI (Italian Alpine Club) red/white paint stripes together with an identifying number – these can be found along the way on signposts, prominent stones, trees, walls and rock faces.

Each walk description is preceded by an information box containing the following essential data:
- **Start**
- **Finish**
- **Distance** in kilometres and miles.
- **Ascent/Descent** Height gain and loss are an indication of effort required and need to be taken into account alongside difficulty and distance when planning the day. Generally speaking, a walker of average fitness will cover 300m (about 1000ft) in ascent in one hour.
- **Difficulty** Each walk has been classified by grade, although adverse weather conditions will make any route more arduous.
  - *Grade 1* Easy route on clear tracks and paths, suitable for beginners.

  - *Grade 2* Paths across hill and mountain terrain, with lots of ups and downs; a reasonable level of fitness is required.
  - *Grade 3* Strenuous, entailing some exposed stretches and possibly prolonged ascent. Experience and extra care are recommended.
- **Walking time** This does not include pauses for picnics, views, photos or nature stops, so always add on a good couple of hours when planning your day. Times given during the descriptions are partial (as opposed to cumulative).
- **Access** Information on how to get to the start point and away from the finish point by public and/or private transport.

Within the walk descriptions, 'path' is used to mean a narrow pedestrian-only way, 'track' and 'lane' are unsurfaced but vehicle width, and 'road' is surfaced and open to traffic unless specified otherwise. Compass bearings are in abbreviated form (N, S, NNW and so on) as are right (R) and left (L). Reference landmarks and places encountered en route and shown on the accompanying map are in **bold** type, with altitude in metres above sea level given as 'm', not to be confused with minutes (abbreviated as min). Note that 100m = 328ft.

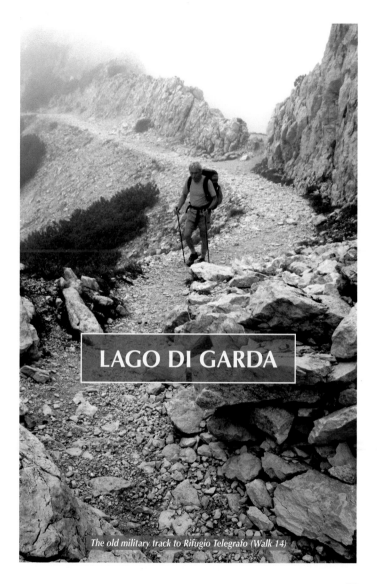

LAGO DI GARDA

The old military track to Rifugio Telegrafo (Walk 14)

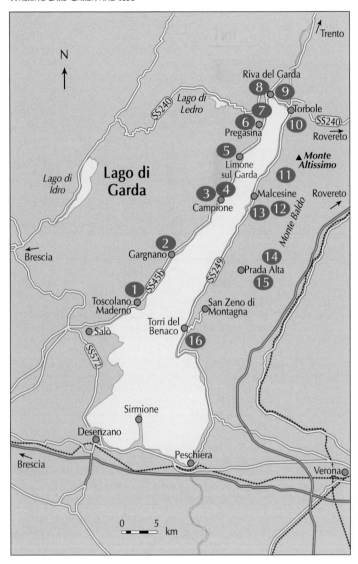

INTRODUCTION

Malcesine's inviting lakefront

Shared between three regions – Lombardia, Trentino and Veneto – magnificent Lago di Garda is blessed with remarkably varied landscapes, from lakeside beaches to soaring mountains. The southern shores are very Mediterranean in flavour, lined with olive groves and vineyards, its glittering waters spreading lazily onto the plains close to the renowned city of Verona. However the most impressive part is the breathtaking northern sweep where the lake is squeezed between dramatic cliffs hundreds of metres high, creating stiff breezes which race across the surface of the water, much to the delight of keen yachtsmen and windsurfers. Towering above it all is the splendid Monte

Baldo massif, a haven for walkers and paragliders.

Garda is the largest lake in Italy with a total surface area of 370km^2, 125km in circumference, 51km in length and 17km across at its widest point. Its old Roman name was 'Benacus' after the god who protected the lake and its inhabitants: a comforting thought.

Its beauty has been appreciated since ancient times when the poet Catullus described it as a 'pearl' – and generations of illustrious writers, artists and musicians have found inspiration and romance here. DH Lawrence eloped to Lake Garda in 1912 with his beloved Frieda. He may have heard about it through the writings of the great German philosopher Johann Wolfgang von Goethe who sang its praises (1786), noting: 'How I wish my friends were here for a moment to enjoy the view I have before me!' They certainly heeded his words, as Lago di Garda has been a summer playground for northern Europeans for centuries. Poor Byron was not so lucky or optimistic and commented grumpily in 1816: 'Terrible weather. Poured with rain. It would have been better not to have come.'

EXPLORING THE LAKE

The southern end of Lago di Garda has two resorts with a distinctly seaside feel: Peschiera (Tourist Info Tel 045 7550810 www.tourismpeschiera. it) and Desenzano (Tel 030 3748726 www.provincia.brescia.it/turismo),

both on the Milan–Verona–Venice railway line. They are good entry points for the lake and have regular ferry services, but lie rather too far south to be useful as a base for walkers. Halfway between the two is the Sirmione peninsula, a spectacular finger of land that terminates with a picturesque castle and a vast ancient Roman resort, the Grotte di Catullo: well worth a visit.

Running up the western edge of the lake is the SS572/SS45b, with plentiful bus services by Arriva/SIA all the way north to Riva del Garda. **Salò**, 22km up, is the first town of interest, a procession of magnificent villas and grand hotels from the late 1700s and 1800s. Many were occupied by Mussolini and his cohorts in 1943 in a last-ditch attempt to keep fascism alive under the short-lived RSI

Gargnano (Walk 2)

Limone and its lemon groves squeezed below soaring cliffs

(Repubblica Sociale Italiana), which struggled on until Italy was liberated by the partisan forces and the Allies in 1945. (A local association organises themed excursions along the western shoreline: visit www.asar-garda.org.)

A further 6km on is **Toscolano Maderno**, where the mid-lake car ferry from Torri del Benaco docks. Its bulging delta, created, over time by the River Toscolano, is a haven for campers. The watercourse was also the reason for the development of paper mills in attractive Valle delle Cartiere, now industrial archaeological sites explored in Walk 1. Of the plentiful hotels there's centrally located Albergo Giardino (Tel 0365 641360 www.albergo-giardino. com) in the traffic-free part of town (Tourist Office Tel 0365 644298 www. prolocotoscolanomaderno.com).

Another 8km north, accessible by Arriva/SIA bus or ferry, is photogenic **Gargnano** that so charmed DH Lawrence with its lemon gardens. They would be covered over with scaffolding and roofed with planks in the cold winter months to protect the precious fruit, and fires lit inside to ward off freezing conditions. The economic peak for the cultivation of lemons was in the mid 1800s; thereafter a disease decimated the crops, while the *coup de grâce* was the discovery of a synthetic form of citric acid, combined with competition from groves on the Amalfi Coast, from which the local industry never recovered. Stay at delightful lakeside Hotel Bartabel (Tel 0365 71330 www.hotelbartabel.it) or Hotel Garni Riviera (Tel 0365 72292 www.garniriviera.it). The Tourist Office is on the main road opposite the bus stop (Tel 0365 791243 www.gargnanosulgarda.it). Walk 2 sets out from here, climbing to the beautiful cliffside Eremo di San Valentino.

The ensuing narrower stretch of the SS45b is responsible for the road's notoriety as it comprises sequences of tunnels bored through lakeside cliffs where drivers have to deal with rapidly alternating sunlight and shade. It was not put through until 1931 as the extremely steep cliffs made road construction challenging to say the least. Film buffs will recognise the road in a car chase from the 2008 James Bond film *Quantum of Solace*.

An abrupt turn-off 11km from Gargnano leads to tiny **Campione** squeezed up against a sheer cliff on a small fan of fluvial detritus. An important industrial centre as early as medieval times, with mills and metal-working enterprises powered by harnessing the impetuous Torrente di San Michele that flows through a dramatic rocky chasm, it had paper and cotton mills in the 1900s when a model village was constructed for the workers. Campione has since been transformed into a smart sailing resort. The lakeside bus service calls in here and Walks 3 and 4 explore the exciting chasm as well as climbing to the hilltop villages. The cafés and grocery shop are useful for walkers as is the modern hostel (Tel 0365 791102 www.campioneunivela.it).

Next en route is absolutely delightful **Limone sul Garda**, likewise constructed right up against the cliffs in a wonderful position overlooking a bay yet protected from prevailing winds and sun drenched year-round. It is crowded with dozens of flourishing terraces which once supported citrus and lemon plantations, as the name would suggest (although scholars insist it derives from either *limen* for 'border' or *lima* for 'river'). JW Goethe wrote this inviting description after a trip by rowing boat: 'We went past Limone, whose mountainside gardens, arranged in terraces and planted with lemon trees, have a rich and well-kept appearance. The whole garden consists of rows of square white pillars, placed at certain intervals, which ascend the mountain in steps.'

Frequent ferries on the Malcesine–Riva del Garda circuit – and many on the complete lake run – call in at the pretty port alongside colourful fishing craft. Lakefront accommodation includes Hotel all'Azzurro (Tel 0365 954000 www.hghotels.com) and Hotel Sole (Tel 0365 954055 www.hotelsolelimone.com). There's a Tourist Office on the main road near the bus stop (Tel 0365 918987 www.visitlimonesulgarda.com). Stay here for Walk 5, a wonderful exploration of the wild Val del Singol. At the time of writing a spectacular cycle track was under construction from Limone heading north around the lake edge. It will also be open to walkers – enquire locally.

The peaceful village of **Pregasina**, accessible from Riva del Garda via a long road tunnel near Lago di Ledro, is visited on Walks 6 and 7 and has aptly named Hotel Panorama (Tel 0464 550993 www.panoramapregasina.it).

At the very top of the lake is the lively market town of **Riva del Garda** with a picturesque traffic-free heart of old streets crammed with shops and houses, overseen by battlements. In the main lakeside square is Hotel Centrale (Tel 0464 552344 www. hotelcentralegarda.it).

Riva has a large bus terminal at the rear of the old town: Trentino Trasporti is responsible for services to Rovereto railway station as well as the rare service to Pregasina; ATV runs down the eastern side of the lake and on to Verona, while Arriva/SIA covers the western shore.

The centrally located Tourist Office is contactable at Tel 0464 554444 www.gardatrentino.it. Walks 7, 8 and 9 begin in Riva.

Torbole occupies the top north-eastern corner of the lake, and lies in the shadow of Monte Altissimo, the northernmost outlier of mammoth Monte Baldo. It has plenty of buses on the Riva–Rovereto and Riva–Verona lines, as well as ferries on the Malcesine–Limone circuit. Walk 10 begins here, close to the Tourist Office (Tel 0464 505177 www.gardatrentino. it). This unassuming lakeside village was the setting for a fascinating tale starring a 15th-century Fitzcarraldo of the Venetian Republic.

A VENETIAN VICTORY

Back in the year 1438 the mighty Venetian Republic was threatened on its western border by the powerful Visconti of the Duchy of Milan, who were extending their control across the Po Plain. In no position to engage in full-scale warfare, Venice devised an ingenious plan: they would surprise the enemy's armada on Lago di Garda by approaching stealthily from the north. The strategic importance of this undertaking is reflected in its astronomical cost – a hefty 15,000 ducats.

A fleet of 33 long boats and galleys set sail from the lagoon to navigate the Adige River to Verona then north via a series of locks, a voyage of 200km. South of Rovereto the craft began the hard part: 25km overland to Torbole dragged by 2000 paired oxen, using tree trunks as rollers for the laborious climb. Hundreds of labourers cleared mountainsides and erected bridges; robust cables and winches ensured a safe passage for the steep descent to the lakeside. Unfortunately the earth-moving operations had not gone unnoticed and the Milanese awaited the Venetians at Desenzano harbour; defeat was inevitable, and only two galleys escaped capture. However, all was not lost. Two years later a new fleet was assembled and victory resounding, thus bringing the entire lake under Venetian control.

Goethe is remembered at Malcesine

Dominated by the colossal bulk of Monte Baldo, the SS249 heads south from Torbole for 14km to the picturesque town of **Malcesine**, its medieval heart still intact. Perched on a rocky promontory, it grew up around a castle erected by the lords of Verona, the Scaligeri. Enjoy the views from the battlements and tower, and render homage to JW Goethe, who risked arrest here in 1786 when his innocent sketching generated suspicions that he was spying for the Hapsburgs! It was during a sojourn at Malcesine in the summer of 1913 that the young Austrian artist Gustav Klimt hired a rowing boat to paint the town from the water in inspiring pastel hues.

The huge range of accommodation includes central Hotel Alpino (Tel 045 7400053 www. hotelalpinomalcesine.com). Frequent ferries and ATV buses on the Verona–Riva del Garda run call in. From May to October a Tourist Bus shuttles back and forth between Malcesine and Cassone (4km away), where you can stay at Hotel Cassone (Tel 045 6584197 www.hotelcassone.com). The helpful main Tourist Office is near the bus stop (Tel 045 7400044 www. visitmalcesine.com).

Monte Baldo, rising high above the town, boasts awesome views. This forbidding limestone barrier runs north–south for 40km, separating Lago di Garda from the Adige valley-cum-traffic artery. It consists of a string of tops: Altissimo, Cima delle Pozzette, Telegrafo and the highest, Valdritta, at 2218m. The massif remained high and dry during the ice ages, a refuge for unique species of alpine flora and earning it the title 'Botanical Garden of Europe'. It can easily be reached thanks to an ultra-modern two-stage cable car from Malcesine, complete with revolving cabins, that glides over the olive groves and up to dizzy Bocca Tratto Spino for Walks 11 or 12.

Whereas Walk 13 begins from the intermediate cable-car station at San Michele where Locanda Monte Baldo offers rooms with a view (Tel 045 7401679 www.locandamontebaldo. com), it is also possible to drive this far up from the lakeside. The lovely southernmost section of Monte Baldo, the best area for wildflower seekers, is accessed from Prada Alta – see below. (**Note** It's best to wait until mid-June to embark on walking routes on Monte Baldo to ensure they are snow-free – check locally.)

About halfway down the eastern shore of Lago di Garda is peaceful **Torri del Benaco** with a pretty harbour and pedestrian-only centre dominated by a medieval castle-museum whose battlements double as a wonderful lake belvedere. It also boasts one of the few working *limonaie* (lemon groves) on Lago di Garda (Tourist Office Tel 045 7225120 www.tourism. verona.it). Torri is well served by ATV buses and frequent car and passenger

Limonaia at Torri del Benaco

ferries across to Toscolano Maderno, though few passenger services around the lake. Set at the port is lovely Hotel Gardesana (Tel 045 7225411 www. gardesana.eu), while less expensive and a short stroll away is Onda Garni (Tel 045 7225895 www.garnionda. com). Walk 16 departs from Torri to explore a clutch of modest rock engravings.

High above at 580m, **San Zeno di Montagna**'s cool air is a great attraction for midsummer holidaymakers. It is linked to Torri del Benaco and Verona by ATV bus runs. The village is strung out along a panoramic ridge, and in summer the air is thick with the divine scent of lime trees. It has a scattering of shops, and a Tourist Office (Tel 045 6289296 www.comunesanzenodimontagna. it); friendly Hotel Centrale Tel 045 7285111 www.bbalbergocentrale. it); Hotel Bellavista (Tel 045 7285286 www.bellavistahotel.eu); and Taxi (Tel 045 7285590, Mob. 337 471658).

The road continues 6km northeast to **Prada Alta** set at 1000m, with the lifts up the eastern flanks of Monte Baldo explored in Walks 14 and 15. There's accommodation at hotel/ campsite Edelweiss (Tel 045 6289039 www.edelweiss-hotel.it), which also runs a well-stocked supermarket. A handy summer Walk&Bike bus organised by ATV from Verona draws in here on an almost daily basis. (**Note** It stops at the car park near the main Chiesa di San Zeno di Montagna, before continuing up to Prada Alta.)

MAPS

Kompass sheet n.102 Lago di Garda, 1:50,000 covers all the walks with varying levels of accuracy. For greater detail, Riva del Garda Tourist Information sells a good 1:30,000 map for Walks 5–10, and Lagiralpina do two excellent 1:25,000 maps – n.12 'Alto Garda' covers Walks 3–13 and n.20 'Monte Baldo' is good for Walks 3, 4 and 12–16. Kompass map n.694 1:25,000 'Parco Alto Garda Bresciano' covers Walks 1 and 2.

TRANSPORT

- ATV buses
  Tel 045 8057922
  www.atv.verona.it
- Ferry timetables
  Tel 800 551801
  www.navlaghi.it
- Malcesine cable car
  www.funiviedelbaldo.it
- Prada Alta lifts
  www.prada-costabella.it
- Arriva/SIA buses
  Tel 840 620001
  www.arriva.it
- Trentino Trasporti buses
  Tel 0461 821000
  www.ttesercizio.it

WALK 1
Valle delle Cartiere

Start/Finish	Ponte Toscolano road bridge
Distance	7.3km (4.5 miles)
Ascent/Descent	400m/400m
Difficulty	Grade 1–2
Walking time	2hr
Access	Toscolano Maderno can be reached by bus or ferry. The road bridge over Torrente Toscolano where the walk starts is on the northern edge of the villages and has a bus stop.

The fascinating Valle delle Cartiere – valley of the paper mills – is hidden away at the rear of the combined Toscolano Maderno villages. As of the 1300s, papermaking flourished here thanks to Torrente Toscolano with around 60 mills operating; the Venetian Republic was an important 15th–16th century client. Times and machinery change; the last mill closed its doors in 1962 and a single mill moved to the lakefront. Modern day visitors are accompanied up the valley by helpful multilingual info boards explaining both history and landscape and a museum (Museo della Carta www.valledellecartiere.it) is well worth a visit. Further up the valley comes a suspended walkway over a gorge before a steep climb to a plateau and stroll through rural Gaino, then a leisurely return to the valley floor.

Note: should the Covoli walkway be closed, before the Luseto footbridge take the old mule track R (SE) up to the bench and shrine (260m) near Gaino, and turn R to slot into the main route.

From the bus stop cross the **Ponte Toscolano** road bridge (65m) and take the first street L curving past the Municipio following signs for Museo della Carta. The minor road for Gaino soon climbs R while you keep straight ahead N along Torrente Toscolano, the way soon unsurfaced. You pass an abandoned mill and hydroelectric plant before short tunnels cut through the soaring cliffs. After a **car park**, a final tunnel is all that separates you from the

The peaceful lakefront at Toscolano

Museo della Carta (the papermaking museum) is well worth a visit

former paper mill now **Museo della Carta** and its riverside café, a worthwhile detour.

The walk proceeds in gentle ascent past the nearby fork (Lupo, 135m) where the return route from Gaino joins up. Bear L over the river to a junction and villa

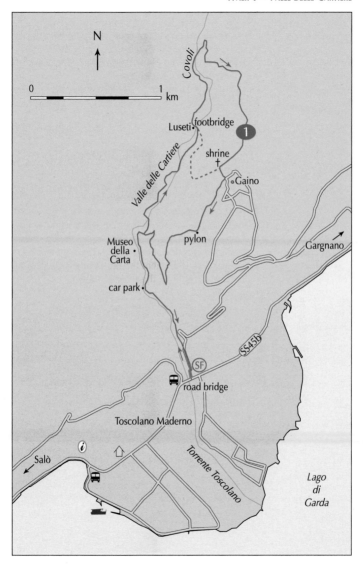

where you keep R, in common with the BVG (Bassa Via del Garda) and n.217. From this point upper Valle delle Cartiere is clearly dominated by pyramidal Monte Castello, while the rocky river banks below host optimistic fishermen. An interesting series of 18th century kilns occupy this area, before a long stone wall and a bridge to the R bank and Caneto with picnic benches, houses and another fork for Gaino. The extensive remains of a mill close to the river are encountered before a **footbridge** takes the path back to the L bank at Luseti. Here it's R on n.279B past Scout Camp premises. At the ensuing fork in woodland keep L on n.220B and you quickly find yourself on a marvellous narrow walkway hanging off the cliff edge through the **Covoli** gorge (50min).

Where the normal path resumes, walk on to join the steep concrete lane climbing R through trees to emerge at a pylon amid fields and small farms. At a wide unsurfaced road branch R (E) on n.279 with bird's-eye views over Valle delle Cartiere, its old mills dwarfed by the dramatic cliff flanks. Heading S through olive groves

Valle delle Cartiere is peppered with remains of old paper mills

The old road in lower Valle delle Cartiere

the quiet road, surfaced here, reaches a signed junction where you go R on Via Giotto (n.217/BVG) and along a high stone wall to a **shrine** and bench (260m, 30min).

Ignore the branch R signed for Valle delle Cartiere and veer L towards the houses of **Gaino**. Take the next R, Via Donatello, which meanders S out of the residential area as a quiet rural lane with some views through to the lake. A large **pylon** marks a fork where you keep R (initially W) for the start of descent through olive groves. At a house continue on a path R in woodland, soon widening to a lane and climbing briefly. Where this splits, go sharp R (NNW) for a leisurely descent on old cobbles past a traffic barrier. Down at the floor of Valle delle Cartiere fork sharp L back past the Museo della Carta and retrace your steps to the walk end at the **road bridge** (40min).

WALK 2
Eremo di San Valentino

Start/Finish	Gargnano bus stop
Distance	10km (6.2 miles)
Ascent/Descent	650m/650m
Difficulty	Grade 2
Walking time	3hr 45min
Access	Gargnano has plenty of buses from Toscolano Maderno; slightly fewer from Riva di Garda and Limone. Ferries also call in. By car you can drive as far as Sasso, cutting the walk time to 1hr 15min.

The Eremo di San Valentino is a magical spot: a tiny church and hermit's dwelling sheltering under a dramatic cliff hanging off a rugged mountain. The modest building is invisible to the naked eye from the lakeside as it blends perfectly into its rocky surroundings. It overlooks Gargnano, a particularly pretty town halfway along the western shore of Lago di Garda and a lovely spot to spend a couple of nights.

Passing the old gardens and orchards at the foot of sheer cliffs, the walk climbs 650m on cobbled lanes and paths through woodland with a distinctly Mediterranean flavour. En route are local shrines known as *santelle*, as well as frequent red/white CAI waymarking. The walk touches on the village of Sasso, an alternative entry point (via rare bus from Gargnano) where the justifiably popular way branches off for the Eremo.

LEMON GROVES

The district is dotted with elegant villas designed for the bourgeoisie of the late 18th to 19th century, alongside flourishing olive groves and splendid traditional *limonaia* plantations. DH Lawrence wrote 'rows of naked pillars rising out of the green foliage like ruins of temples: white square pillars of masonry, standing forlorn in their colonnades and squares, rising up from the mountain-sides here and there, as if they remained from some great race that had once worshipped here'. Many of these old agricultural properties have been converted into residences with wonderful gardens.

From the bus stop on the main road opposite the Tourist Office at **Gargnano** (66m), follow the sign for 'passaggio pedonale' down steps by a car park. This quickly brings you onto the walkway that leads L (NE) along the lake's edge, a lovely start to this route. At the charming port and ferry wharf go L across **Piazza Feltrinelli** to pick up Via Roma R. Beneath elegant palaces, continue to **Piazza Vittorio Veneto** and branch L up Via Parrocchia. Steps lead up to a water distributor alongside a huge pink colonnaded church, set on the main road. To the R a matter of metres on the opposite side of the road is a bus stop and map board (15min), and the start of Via Crocefisso, waymarked red/white for CAI n.30. Soaring almost

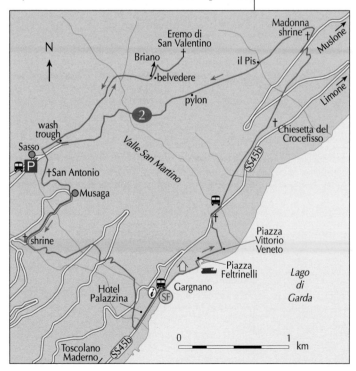

The walk follows the lakeside at Gargnano

overhead is the pale mountain outcrop where the Eremo nestles, before rising to Monte Comer.

Moving off NNE the cobbled lane makes a gentle, steady ascent screened by stone walls retaining the marvellous terraced gardens of lemons, olives and grapes which spill out over the way, accompanied by straggling bouquets of caper plants. Interesting information boards are set along the route. The tiny yellow **Chiesetta del Crocefisso** is passed, and you soon cross the road for Muslone. As the way steepens, there are plenty of opportunities for drinking in views east across the lake to the heights of Monte Baldo. A curve L sees you heading up through wood to the road once more.

Fork R along the asphalt for a matter of metres to where a lane resumes past a showy majolica **Madonna shrine**. Not far up you fork L (SW) on n.30 for a steep stretch that leads through woods to an overhang and dry white torrent bed, **il Pis** (303m). Here the lane ends at a house, and a path takes over for steeper rocky walking W. At a power line and **pylon**, and an excellent lookout, a variant route turns sharp R – experts only as it entails an exposed scramble – but you proceed L under bright red cliffs. The way soon follows old stone terracing, then joins a lane near a house and Valle San Martino. It's not far up to a group of new houses, where you branch R on tarmac.

Only minutes uphill is the laid-back village of **Sasso** (520m, 1hr) looking over to twin peaks Monte Castello and Pizzocolo. However, before you reach the village centre fork R on Via Sasso (aka n.31), and R again at the **wash trough**. An old paved way leaves the settlement NE, climbing easily through shady woodland to a superb **belvedere** with bird's-eye views to Gargnano, Monte Baldo opposite, and down the sweep of the lake to the Sirmione peninsula. Ignore the fork L for Briano, and keep R, soon to plunge down a gully on good steps. The path then leads L around to a door – push it open and up the staircase to the divine hideout of the **Eremo di San Valentino**

The rock overhang at Eremo di San Valentino

(712m, 40min). Cypress trees shield the tiny church and rooms built onto the overhanging rock face. A true place for meditation.

> In 1630 the plague struck and claimed 400 victims. The remaining population fled to the mountainous hinterland for refuge; once the 'all clear' sounded and people could return to their lakeside homes, survivors built the church of the **Eremo di San Valentino** in gratitude. In 1842 it reportedly became the hideout for a local man avoiding military call-up.

Afterwards – duly refreshed – retrace your steps, but at the **wash trough** keep straight on to the square of **Sasso** (520m, 35min), with a café. If you don't time your arrival for one of the rare buses that link with Gargnano, then fork L at the handy map board and soon R, flanking a playing field (n.19). This lane soon curves L below the **Chiesa di San Antonio** with breathtaking views across the glittering lake that will take your mind off the near-vertical descent towards the rooftops of **Musaga** (454m). Red/white markings lead down through alleys in the well-kept village.

After veering R down through a covered passageway, a short stretch L (SW) leads along a little-used road. At a prominent **shrine** branch L (E) on n.37, the concrete lane Via al Pastore. This leads in rapid descent past farms and across the road for a steep stony path. After a further road crossing it becomes Via dei Mulini, once home to numerous water-powered mills. Steps lead past a sequence of houses to a concrete lane. The gradient finally eases a little as you veer R across a stream and cut over the road once more. A narrow path takes over, flanked by stone walls. This brings you out on tarmac near **Hotel Palazzina** and shortly at the main lakeside road, where you go L for the short distance back to the bus stop at **Gargnano** (66m, 1hr).

WALK 3

Campione to Pregasio Loop

Start/Finish	Campione, Piazza Arrighini
Distance	9.7km (6 miles)
Ascent/Descent	670m/670m
Difficulty	Grade 2
Walking time	4hr
Access	A short detour off the SS45b as it passes through tunnels between Gargnano and Limone, Campione is served by Arriva/SIA buses, as is Pregasio (an alternative entry or exit point). No ferries call in at Campione.

Campione is an amazing spot, a cluster of historic factories set on a tiny alluvial fan 'island' beneath sheer cliffs that soar a good 500m skywards. Now a low-key resort for sailing and windsurfing enthusiasts, it offers a couple of cafés and restaurants, along with a modest supermarket. Walk 4 also begins at Campione.

This is an exhilarating circuit that climbs high above the dramatic cliffs. Both start and finish sections follow long flights of steps dug out of the cliff face to penetrate the dramatic ravine where the Torrente San Michele has spent centuries wearing away the limestone and sculpting a deep narrow course. Its waters have been exploited since medieval times as a source of power for industry at Campione. The path goes through a 200m-long tunnel, with minimal electric lighting; take a torch or headlamp. The middle section wanders through peaceful farmland hundreds of metres above the lake, touching on villages such as Pregasio. **Note:** path numbering is undergoing changes so there may be discrepancies between the description and what's on the ground.

From centrally located Piazza Arrighini at **Campione** (67m), take the footbridge S across Torrente San Michele, and then R (SW) up steps marked as n.110/267. This leads over a road for the start of the fascinating old route that climbs steeply, aided by a handrail. It passes beneath

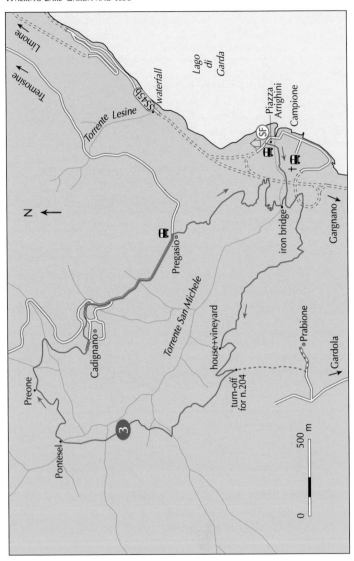

water conduits on arched supports as the ravine of the Torrente San Michele plunges far below. The path goes through a low rock tunnel with some lighting – watch your head! – and emerges into daylight again to follow man-made canals and pools.

Ignore the R fork across the **iron bridge** (30min, the return route) and keep L on n.266. Initially SW this quickly becomes a superbly spectacular path close to the cliff edge with brilliant views over Lago di Garda from Monte Baldo and Malcesine to Campione at your feet. Bearing R (W) it levels out, entering woodland thick with smoke bush and hornbeam. A little way in, take care not to miss the **turn-off R for n.204** signed for Pontesel.

> A short detour from the turn-off is the village of **Prabione** and the Visitor Centre of the Parco Alto Garda Bresciano (Tel 0365 761049 www.cm-parcoaltogarda.bs.it).

It's a gentle descent through chestnut woodland with lovely views back to the ravine and the lake beyond. At a modest vineyard and small house, fork L up a lane for a short winding climb to join a broader lane, still n.204 (500m). This proceeds N in gradual descent past another modest house and narrows to a path that drops decisively through woodland to the amazing cleft gorge crossed by the tiniest stone bridge that is **Pontesel**, aka Ponticello (290m, 1hr 30min).

Rural landscape on the way to Pontesel

*The chasm at
Pontesel*

The clear path continues through dense jungle-like vegetation with masses of ferns, occasionally along natural limestone ledges, finally reaching a rural landscape and cultivated fields. Follow red/white waymarks up to a Y-junction (**Preone**) where you fork R on n.203. The level lane heads essentially SE to flank olive plantations before joining the tarmac at **Cadignano**.

It's not far downhill to the village of **Pregasio** (477m, 50min), with cafés and a bus service. At the start of the buildings, turn R immediately opposite the supermarket down Via Lomas – ignore the archway and fork R at house n.10 down steps and past a gate, then L at the corner of the garden. A path leads down to a lane, n.110/267 heading SE in a rural landscape of olive groves and orchards. At the forks take care to follow the red/white markings. At the edge of the wood, don't miss the fork L onto a path through oak woods and soon a long stretch hewn into the rock face with a guiding steel cable. This descends into the ravine on a thrilling cliffside path, climbs over a central outcrop and finally reaches the **iron bridge** (50min) encountered on the way up.

From here, return to the lakeside and **Campione** (67m, 20min) by reversing your outward route.

Campione at the foot of cliffs

WALK 4
Campione to Pieve Loop

Start/Finish	Univela Hostel, Campione
Distance	8.3km (5.1 miles)
Ascent/Descent	780m/780m
Difficulty	Grade 2
Walking time	3hr
Access	A short detour off the SS45b as it passes through tunnels between Gargnano and Limone, Campione has no ferries but is served by SIA/Arriva buses. **Note:** at the time of writing there were two separate bus stops at Campione – one for each direction. Check locally.
	The hostel where the walk starts is located near the road tunnel at the northern end of the settlement.

From Campione as you look north the eye is drawn up the breathtakingly sheer cliff faces that seem to lean over the lakefront. Good eyes will make out the tiny buildings belonging to the village of Pieve di Tremosine, all but hanging off the edge at a dizzy 432 metres. Amazingly, a centuries-old, near-vertical path climbs up there, hewn out of the rock face by the ingenious inhabitants to lug goods to and from the tiny port below. With the advent of the industrial age, help came in the shape of two ingenious lifts: the 1898 (to 1918) cableway activated by a counterweight consisting of stones, then the 1907 (until 1931) lift activated by water. In 1913 a road to the village was finally excavated through the nearby white-knuckle narrow Forra ravine and defined by Winston Churchill 'the eighth wonder of the world'.

Not for the weak-kneed or faint of heart due to lots of steps up and down and a few dizzy stretches, this exhilarating circuit takes the old path to Pieve then loops back to Campione via farmland and the dramatic ravine of San Michele, also visited in Walk 3. A torch is handy for the tunnel towards the end. This walk is unsuitable in bad weather as it could be dangerous.

Note: path numbering is undergoing changes in this area so there may be discrepancies between the description, local signs and maps.

From the **Univela Hostel** at **Campione** (65m) a signpost
for path n.150 points you behind the hostel and up steps
to an old traffic-free lakefront road overlooking the sailing centre. Enjoying marvellous views across the water
to Monte Baldo towering over Malcesine, you proceed N
at the foot of the awesome cliffs and through short tunnels. Gentle ascent leads to a fork where you keep L (as
per red/white waymarks) up a lane and under a waterfall
(Torrente Lesine). Cypress trees accompany a short section
above the main road. As tarmac is reached (the road to
Pieve), branch L as indicated and walk along the narrow
pavement to the turn-off R for the resumption of n.150
and more brilliant lake views. Don't miss the neck-craning
view of Pieve di Tremosine almost directly overhead now!

    Enjoy the leisurely gradient as further you're pointed
L (NW) for the start of the testing stone steps and pathway
(n.141). (Ignore the fork R unless you're attracted by the
15min drop to the old lakeside port). Through evergreen

*Campione and its
cliffs are admired
from the old
lakeside road*

47

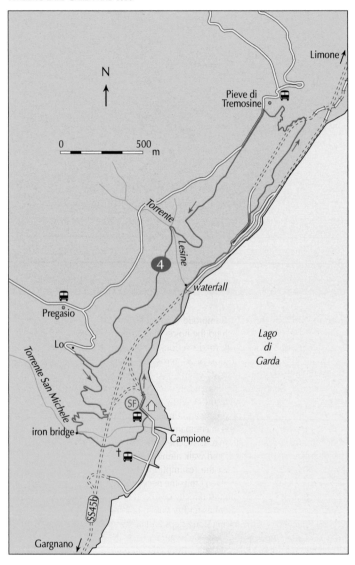

oak wood it's up and up on a winding stony way, often cut out of the rock face with a protective cable. Further up is a Madonna shrine at a cave followed by the final zigzags with reinforced stone walls that conclude at the breathtaking Cimaporto terrace of **Pieve di Tremosine** (432m, 1hr 15min) with cafés, eateries and groceries.

At Piazza Cozzaglio go L on Via IV novembre as far as the church where you take the stepped way with cypresses up to the war memorial. Keep L to join the road past a bus stop then Hotel Paradiso (with a famous belvedere terrace). Immediately afterwards fork L (SSW) on quiet Via Vagne (n.142) past a playing field and into olive groves in constant descent and across the Lesine valley. As an unsurfaced lane, it concludes at a house

A shrine and cave are a good excuse for a breather en route to Pieve di Tremosine

– keep R on the marked path up through chestnut wood and over a shoulder through terraced olives. This leads through to the path junction of **Lo** (424m, 45min) – go sharp L on the concreted lane n.110 (in common with Walk 3 now). Wide curves lead in descent past a lookout point and through well-kept fields and olive trees. Where light woodland resumes take care not to miss the faintly marked fork sharp L (E) for a narrow stony path. This wastes no time plunging via rocky steps and along thrilling cliff ledges with steel cable. After a climb over a central outcrop you drop into the dramatic ravine of Torrente San Michele to cross an **iron bridge** near water channels.

A steep cliff-hugging path descends to the lake and Campione

Ignore the fork for Tignale, and continue L along to the dimly lit tunnel – watch your head on the rocky ceiling. A long series of knee-jarring concrete steps past minor hydroelectric works drop to the former industrial area of Campione. Turn L at the bottom to cross the footbridge over Torrente San Michele and into **Piazza Arrighini** with cafés and restaurants. To return to the Hostel, go straight ahead (N) to the lakeside then L (1hr).

The church at Campione is backed by steep cliffs

WALK 5

Limone sul Garda and the Valle del Singol

Start/Finish	Limone sul Garda, Info Point
Distance	10km (6.2 miles)
Ascent/Descent	880m/880m
Difficulty	Grade 3
Walking time	4hr 30min
Access	Limone sul Garda can be reached by ferry as well as and buses from Riva del Garda (Trentino Trasporti) and Gargnano and southern towns (Arriva/SIA).

A wonderfully rewarding circuit for walkers with good stamina and path-tested knees, climbing high into beautiful and craggy Val del Singol. Enjoy a picnic on the higher central section before an exhilarating plunge down steep and rocky Val Pura. The walk starts and concludes in the attractive lakeside village of Limone sul Garda, beset with *limonaie*, abandoned lemon terraces now reminiscent of ancient temples.

The walk has several narrow Grade 3 central sections that are both steep and exposed at times, and walking boots with a good grip are recommended. This route should be avoided in bad weather as it may be dangerous. That said, a simple stroll up the lane in Valle del Singol is always worthwhile.

At **Limone sul Garda** (66m) from the lakeside **Info Point** turn uphill on the steps of Via Rovina, then follow the narrow paved road that proceeds up to the main road Via IV Novembre. A short distance left is the main bus stop close to Bar Turista and the main Tourist Office. Straight over is pedestrian-only Via Milanesa, with red/white marking for path n.101. The cobbled way proceeds through the residential area and between old lemon terraces, their walls dripping with caper vines.

Go under an old arch to **Bar La Milanesa** and soon cross a bridge over Torrente San Giovanni. No traffic is allowed beyond this point in beautiful Valle del Singol:

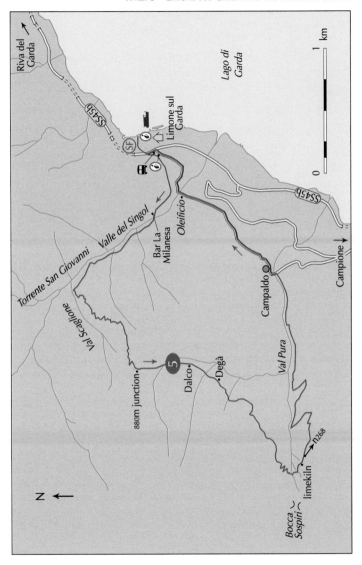

Clear views of Limone during the ascent of Val Scaglione

its apt name means 'narrow, drawing in'. Heading NW after a waterfall and a limekiln, ignore the n.111 fork L for Dalco and stick to the lane, soon to a drinking-water point (Acqua del Singol). The stream cascades alongside the lane, while well beyond, inland, are soaring crags: Préals, Corno Vecchia and Traversole.

Fork L (460m, 45min) on path n.102 up Val Scaglione through conifer woodland and heather. You climb SW above a dry stony streambed to a shoulder, the terrain more and more dramatic with every step. The lakeside township of Limone is seen clearly below on its alluvial fan created by the mountain stream flowing down Valle del Singol.

About halfway up is a short exposed ledge, then the zigzagging resumes and you finally emerge at a welcome clearing and **path junction** (880m, 1hr 15min). Bear L (S) on n.110 to a house and the ruined church at **Dalco** (842m). A gentle uphill stretch SW follows the clear old path to two houses in a lovely setting amid beech and huge conifers. The sunken path now continues to the signed junction of **Degà** (904m, 30min), where you need n.268 for Limone.

With a brilliant lake panorama you soon find yourself plunging SW on a clear if narrow and madly zigzagging path across scree gullies beneath Bocca Sospiri. A wider track is gained at a memorial plaque and **limekiln**, and you soon need to leave n.268 to fork L (E) on n.123, a narrow steep path down wild Val Pura, reminiscent of the wilder scenery of the Dolomites. The curves help take some of the sting out of the abrupt descent. The torrent is crossed further down and a concreted lane joined to lead to the houses of **Campaldo** (220m, 1hr 15min).

Here turn L along a surfaced road in steady descent NE. At an intersection keep L past the former lemon orchard, now labelled 'Casa natale' (birthplace) San Daniele Comboni, a local missionary. Take the lower road here downhill past an **oleificio** (olive press) and a grocery shop at a three-way junction – keep L across Torrente San Giovanni close to the opening of Valle del Singol. Over a rise and down Via Caldogno and you're back at the Tourist Office on the main road near the bus stop at Bar Turista. It's not far back to the lakeside at **Limone sul Garda** (66m, 45min), the perfect place for a well-deserved refreshing drink.

Limone's lovely lakeside

WALK 6
Monte Nodice and Pregasina

Start/Finish	Bus stop 'Bivio per Pregasina' (Pregasina turn-off) near Biacesa
Distance	8.5km (5.3 miles)
Ascent/Descent	600m/600m
Difficulty	Grade 2–3 (Grade 3 section avoidable)
Walking time	3hr 10min
Access	From Riva del Garda take the Trentino Trasporti bus for Molino di Ledro to the first stop after the road tunnel, where a minor road forks L for Pregasina.

A wonderful circuit that takes in a fascinating – albeit modest – mountain, 859m Monte Nodice. As its alternative name Cima di Lé (peak of the lake) suggests, it rises from the very edge of the lake, ensuring exciting views that reach north to embrace the Alps beyond the spectacular expanse of Lago di Garda. The path passes evidence of wartime structures then goes through the beautifully located village of Pregasina, where the cafés do a roaring trade with walkers. After a short leg of tarmac comes the old pot-holed road, reserved for pedestrains and cyclists these days on its crazy winding plunge to Torrente Ponale, accompanied by stunning views.

Energetic souls who make an early start can combine this route with Walk 7, part of which can also be used as a variant return route for Walk 6.

The mountain is riddled with **military structures** dating back to the pre-World War I period when the region belonged to the Austro-Hungarian Empire. These take the shape of trenches and an amazing diagonal stone staircase up a natural cleft ledge.

◀ From the bus stop turn L (E) along the surfaced road for Pregasina to the well-signed start of path n.429 (340m). Prepare for the well-graded climb through woodland on a clear path SE with plentiful red/white waymarks. The uphill pace is steady; after several lines of overgrown trenches the way steepens with loose stones underfoot,

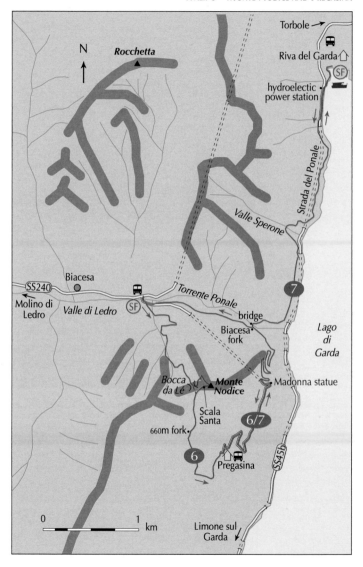

The Scala Santa leading down from Monte Nodice

If you don't have a head for heights and prefer to avoid the dizzy stretches, from Bocca da Lé proceed straight ahead, in descent (S) to pick up the Pregasina path.

finally reaching the saddle **Bocca da Lé** (800m, 1hr 10min). Ignore the path branch R but soon keep L on an unmarked path for good lake views from military structures and a cave. ◀

Keep L then R following red dots to clamber up a rock face W, with some exposure – take special care here. It quickly leads to a wide ledge at a cavern and well-placed benches on a breathtaking belvedere platform with dizzying views down Lago di Garda and a bird's-eye view over the village of Pregasina. Now the path drops a tad, and soon there's a detour to the L along more trenches to amazing views from modest **Monte Nodice** (859m, 10min), up the top of the lake and the Sarca valley beyond Riva del Garda and Torbole. Retrace your steps to where the red dots point downwards on a narrow path for the **Scala Santa** (holy staircase!), a spectacular flight of steps cut into the rock face, equipped with a cable handrail.

It zigzags down past caverns, and veers R through a cleft in the rock and along SW to soon rejoin the main path from Bocca da Lé. Proceeding S, watch your step on the loose stones. At 660m, fork L onto path n.422, soon steep and concreted in parts. Down at a minor road, branch L to the **Chiesa di Pregasina** (532m, 40min), beautifully placed at the foot of Monte Nodice and a superb inspiring outlook across the lake. Stick to the road down past Hotel Panorama with its inviting café-terrace. Past fields and Albergo Rosalpina the surfaced way N narrows, en route to the Regina Mundi **Madonna statue** at Brion (390m, 20min).

The Regina Mundi statue below Pregasina

This superb **platform** is a great place for admiring the windsurfers and sailing boats zipping by on the lake at your feet, backed by lopsided Monte Brione.

The road soon enters a tunnel, but you fork R on the old route, now free of traffic (apart from cyclists). It zigzags madly in descent, the surface badly eroded in parts. By all means take the 'pedonale' (pedestrian) shortcuts, though be warned that they are steep and stony. Bearing L (NNW) under a cliff, the way approaches Torrente Ponale and its valley. Keep your eyes skinned for the **Biacesa fork** L (25min), which leaves the old road to head inland (W), unless you wish to continue to Riva del Garda as follows.

Variant: Strada del Ponale return to Riva del Garda (1hr)
To carry on to Riva del Garda, stick to the old road that soon crosses a **bridge** then curves around the dramatic cliff line en route to Riva del Garda – see Walk 7.

The 'Sentiero del Ponale', which follows the valley inland, takes its name from the river. A lovely paved way heading W into woodland, it is hewn out of the rock here. After a shrine a milestone from 1746 is passed, evidence of the historical importance of the lane, which levels out here. ◄ On the opposite bank runs a historic road built in the 1840s to link the villages in the Lago di Ledro valley with Riva del Garda – see Walk 7. The path turns R onto the modern road for Pregasina; only minutes along is the path fork for n.429, then the bus stop (45min) on the Riva–Molino road.

On the opposite bank runs a historic road built in the 1840s to link the villages in the Lago di Ledro valley with Riva del Garda – see Walk 7.)

WALK 7

Strada del Ponale to Pregasina

Start/Finish	Riva del Garda ferry wharf
Distance	12km (7.5 miles)
Ascent/Descent	470m/470m
Difficulty	Grade 1
Walking time	4hr 15min
Access	Riva del Garda can be reached by ferry and buses from Rovereto (Trentino Trasporti), Verona (ATV) and the western shore (Arriva/SIA).

On the northwestern shore of Lago di Garda steep limestone cliffs plunge hundreds of metres to the glittering waters below. Such geography makes for difficult access, and road builders were true pioneers, hewing lengthy stretches through mountainsides.

This walk, partly along the old Strada del Ponale, is suitable for every level of ability. A series of tunnels is traversed, well illuminated by natural daylight. A note of warning: keep young children well away from the precipitous edges. After the Ponale valley is crossed, the way is surfaced all the way to Pregasina, but is traffic-free as far as the Madonna statue. Pregasina has a couple of cafés and simple restaurants for lunch. There is a bus service from Riva del Garda but runs are few and far between – check with the Tourist Office beforehand. Allow plenty of extra time for photographs and admiring the spectactular views on this walk!

The **Strada del Ponale** was the inspiration of entre-preneur Giacomo Cis in the 1840s to link his home village on Lago di Idro with Riva; alas he died only days before he could see it open in 1851. Today's traffic uses a tunnel on the SS45b below, enabling walkers and mountain bikers to share the simply magnificent – albeit pot-holed – track.

Many tunnels are encountered on the Strada del Ponale

See map for Walk 6.

◀ From the ferry wharf at **Riva del Garda** (65m) walk away from the town along the pavement of the SS45b, aka Gardesana. You pass the historic **hydroelectric power station**, its façade bearing an imposing 1931 statue of the 'Genio delle Acque', the 'God of the Waters', so dubbed by the Italian poet Gabriele D'Annunzio. Just before the main road enters a tunnel fork R up to the start of the Strada del Ponale, and you are plunged straight into the first short **tunnel**, alive with swallows. Weaving in and out of the folds in the mountainside the lane climbs almost imperceptibly among cliffs studded with bright wildflowers, while the new road can occasionally be glimpsed below.

The second tunnel follow soon after; another features World War I military works including lookout posts peeking out of the rock face. After the fourth **tunnel** you swing briefly inland to cross the stream in Valle Sperone and ignore a path fork in the direction of a *via ferrata*. Further along you overlook a derelict hotel terrace high above an abandoned port. The road is surfaced but traffic-free as it enters a valley where the Torrente Ponale forms an attractive waterfall.

As the old road forks R for the Valle di Ledro, go L (sign for Pregasina) across the **bridge** (1hr). Ignore the **fork** R for Biacesa and you soon come across the first of the optional short (but steep) cuts marked 'pedonale' (pedestrian). In any case there are countless wide zigzags that give you time to appreciate the engineering feat. Trees are gradually colonising the old road, their roots breaking up the surface and their branches shading walkers.

As you approach the modern road at a tunnel exit a path cuts up L to the huge Regina Mundi **Madonna statue** (390m, 1hr) at the magnificent lookout. Now it's 1.5km and 100m uphill on the narrow road shared with cars to the relaxed rural setting of **Pregasina** (532m, 30min). The village enjoys wonderful views to the head of the lake with the Sarca delta, not to mention lopsided Monte Brione. The Altissimo and Monte Baldo account for the eastern horizon opposite.

Return the same leisurely way to **Riva del Garda** (65m, 1hr 45min).

The Strada del Ponale cuts the cliff face high above the lake and the road

WALK 8

The Venetian Bastione

Start/Finish	Riva del Garda ferry wharf
Distance	4.5km (2.8 miles)
Ascent/Descent	320m/320m
Difficulty	Grade 1
Walking time	1hr 30min (+ extra 1hr 20min for Santa Barbara)
Access	Riva del Garda can be reached by ferry and buses from Rovereto (Trentino Trasporti), Verona (ATV) and the western shore (Arriva/SIA).

The walk is a loop route, short and sweet, a pleasant way to spend an hour or so. There's also a café at the Bastione. The route can be extended uphill to the chapel at Santa Barbara, a further 325m in ascent, returning the same way. The chapel is a landmark for the town as it is lit up every evening and stands out like a beacon on the mountainside, appearing to float high over the lake. It was built in 1935 by miners working on the hydroelectric power station at Riva del Garda.

RIVA DEL GARDA

The lakeside township preserves a host of reminders of its time under the dominion of the Serenissima Republic of Venice, including a monumental town gate and the Bastione, a sturdy tower erected in the early 16th century on the lower reaches of Monte Rocchetta. Though it was deliberately razed to the ground by French troops in 1703, the council has recently seen fit to restore this photogenic structure. It occupies a fantastic position overlooking the upper lake and a stunning panorama of red-tiled roofs and clustered houses in the town's maze of medieval and Renaissance streets.

From the ferry wharf at **Riva del Garda** (65m) turn inland and cross **Piazza 3 Novembre**, passing the elegant Municipio building. On the corner with Hotel Portici turn R along Via Fiume past houses and shops. This leads

out of the pedestrian *centro storico* via the 11th-century gate **Porta San Marco**, aptly named for the patron saint of Venice.

The Venetian Bastione

Turn L on Via Bastione and L again at the Gardacar building up to the main road SS45b, aka Gardesana. Cross over to the sign for the continuation of Via Bastione, now a surfaced lane heading uphill W. Tight zigzags lead past villas and delightful terraced gardens bursting with all manner of luxuriant vegetation. Inviting benches occupy strategic spots along the way. At a signed fork, keep L for the **Bastione** (210m, 30min). The partially restored tower doubles as a magnificent belvedere, the adjoining café an added bonus.

From the rear of the structure go up path n.404, a series of steps

A bird's-eye view of Riva del Garda from the Bastione

climbing through thick conifer woodland. Around 15min on is a dirt forestry trail and a signed junction (350m), and the extension to Santa Barbara.

Extension to Santa Barbara (1hr 20min return)

Go L to a fork, then R for the signed climb to a hut Capanna Santa Barbara (560m) and the start of a climbing route (which you ignore). A little further along S is the tiny landmark chapel of **Santa Barbara** (625m), a superb spot. Return to the forestry trail to continue with the walk.

Go R along the **forestry trail**, a level route heading N. Where it reaches a concrete lane fork R downhill through woodland dotted with Mediterranean plants. Rather steep at times – to the joy of mountain bikers – it passes another link to the Bastione and plunges towards road level. As the first houses are encountered, branch R on a paved pedestrian-only way down to the Englovacanza B&B. Go R down to the main road (Gardesana), and R again to the Gardacar where you branch L to resume the walk back into the *centro storico* via Porta San Marco and from there to the ferry wharf at **Riva del Garda** (65m, 45min).

WALK 9

Monte Brione

Start/Finish	Riva del Garda, Piazza 3 Novembre
Distance	7.5km (4.7 miles)
Ascent/Descent	300m/300m
Difficulty	Grade 1–2
Walking time	2hr 15min
Access	Riva del Garda can be reached by ferry and buses from Rovereto (Trentino Trasporti), Verona (ATV) and the western shore (Arriva/SIA).

Monte Brione is a curious inclined slab that rises from the otherwise flat northern edge of Lago di Garda, resembling a lopsided layered sponge cake. The western slope hosts a massive olive grove whose light-coloured foliage contrasts with the dark greens of the evergreen Mediterranean vegetation. Monte Brione was the focus of a sprawling system of defensive forts erected by the Austro-Hungarian Empire from the mid-1800s through to World War I, after which the region became the Trentino and part of Italy.

This is a lovely straightforward walk; take a picnic. The lakefront promenade is followed by a steady climb on a stepped path. Wonderful lake and alpine views accompany walkers to the string of forts. After extensive restoration, Forte Garda is now open to the public so allow extra time to explore its inner recesses.

At **Riva del Garda** (65m) from the lakefront **Piazza 3 Novembre** take the *lungolago* lakefront pedestrian promenade ESE. Through parks with comical duck colonies and past a modest beach, it reaches a marina and **Porto San Nicolò** (20min). At the old stone fort (1860–62) turn L up steps with a wooden handrail. This brings you to a surfaced road (Via Monte Brione) and a sign pointing R for the long-distance Sentiero della Pace (path of peace), which you follow.

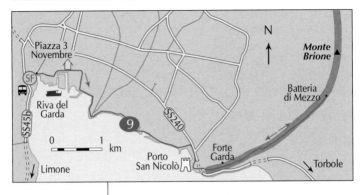

A stepped path at first, it climbs steadily through holm oak and cypress trees following the edge of the crest curving NE. Concrete bunkers are passed belonging to **Forte Garda** that dates back to 1907. Well-placed benches encourage appreciation of superb views over Torbole and its tribe of windsurfers, the Sarca river and its inland fish farms, and the delta where blue-brown waters

The walk begins with a pleasant stroll along the waterfront

View from Monte Brione through olive trees to the Riva hinterland

mix, and beyond to sprawling Monte Baldo. The going is breathtaking, but it gets even better with every step! At olive groves keep R on to the 1900 fortress **Batteria di Mezzo** (332m, 1hr 15min), a position that regales vast views over the Riva del Garda hinterland. ▶

Return to **Riva del Garda** (65m, 1hr) the same way.

The true top of Monte Brione is further north, and studded with antennas. The path is interrupted by fencing, though a narrow slippery route can be taken.

WALK 10
Torbole to Tempesta

Start	Torbole ferry wharf
Finish	Tempesta bus stop
Distance	6.3km (4 miles)
Ascent/Descent	270m/270m
Difficulty	Grade 2
Walking time	2hr 10min
Access	Torbole can be reached by ferry and buses from Riva del Garda and Rovereto (Trentino Trasporti), or Verona (ATV). The ferry wharf is on the southern edge, just south of the Tourist Office. An ATV bus covers the return stretch.

The lower northern reaches of Monte Baldo are explored on this exciting and highly panoramic walk. Courtesy of the Forestry Commission (as part of a forest fire prevention project) a *sentiero attrezzato* is followed, a clear path fitted with well-secured raised iron walkways and ladder-staircases crossing two precipitous outcrops on a wild inaccessible mountainside: almost 400 steps are negotiated in descent. There is no dangerous exposure, and handrails are present at all times. At times it feels like Corsica, with typical *maquis*-like plants and the sight of the sparkling blue 'Mediterranean Sea'!

Towards the end there is an optional return loop on a forestry track instead of descending to Tempesta and the bus back to Torbole. Check times beforehand as an hour may pass between runs.

An amazing **tale of intrigue and stealth** was played out here in the 15th century. The Venetians were losing territory to the Milanese, and craftily transported boats overland to launch them in the lake – see the Lago di Garda Introduction to read more!

From the ferry wharf at **Torbole** (56m), turn L to Hotel Ifigenia and go R on Via Pescicoltura for the 'scalinata'. The flight of steps in question is first R (E), and will see

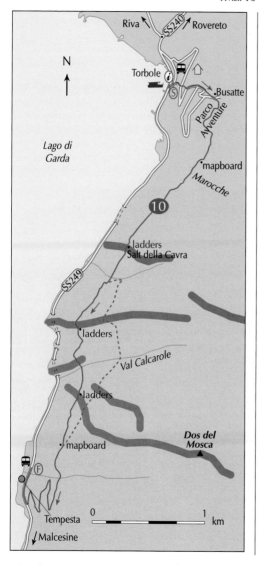

you puffing uphill. Then cross over the road and continue in the same direction up through a park. This ends at a road near a cliff face – keep uphill past Hotel Villa Gloria. A path soon short-cuts through the wood to a car park and lane.

Turn sharp R here to the sign 'Sentiero Panoramico Busatte–Tempesta' that leads straight through the **Busatte Parco Avventure** (201m). After a bike track layout you descend slightly to fork L on a gravel lane. Heading uphill through woodland, it curves under cliffs entering the Marocche, an ancient 'rock glacier' dotted with chaotically fallen slabs and boulders. The official start of

Walker on the sequence of steep ladders crossing wild bushland

the Busatte–Tempesta route is soon announced by a map board (40min). This also doubles as a lovely belvedere taking in the head of the lake with Riva del Garda and the neighbouring cliffs with, clearly visible, the horizontal line of the Strada del Ponale (see Walk 7).

Follow the arrow straight on to the well-kept path S, fitted with benches and information panels. The vegetation is essentially Mediterranean, dominated by holm oak and brightened with rockroses. It's not far along to the first of the exciting **ladder-staircases** (116 steps), essential to get around the aptly named outcrop **Salt della Cavra** ('goat leap'). The wonderfully scenic path then proceeds to the **second set of ladders**, even longer and more thrilling, down sheer cliffs on Corno del Bò (238 steps).

A brief uphill stretch and you're at the **third and final set of ladders** across Val Calcarole (33 steps). At a lane, a map board marking the end of the official path is soon reached (1hr), also showing a variant return.

Return variant (1hr 40min)
By branching L up the lane for an uphill section, you can loop back to rejoin the outward path between the first and second ladders. Thereafter retrace your steps via the **Busatte Parco Avventure** and back down to **Torbole**.

Turn R down the lane in wide curves with views across the lake to Limone. When you reach the roadside, turn R along the SS249 for 5min to the bus stop at **Tempesta** (36m, 30min), where there is nothing in the way of a village; for lakeside cafés return to Torbole.

WALK 11
Monte Baldo: Ventrar to San Michele

Start	Bocca Tratto Spino cable-car station
Finish	San Michele cable-car station
Distance	11.2km (7 miles)
Descent	1160m
Difficulty	Grade 2–3
Walking time	3hr (+ 30min for cable car)
Access	Malcesine is reached by ferry or ATV bus from Torbole or Torri del Benaco and Verona; the *funivia* (cable car) station is very close to the town centre. It is possible to drive to San Michele.

Beginning with a thrilling ride on the ultra-modern Malcesine *funivia* (cable car), this excellent route strikes out along the panoramic top of Monte Baldo via the Colma di Malcesine, an isolated crest with marvellous all-round views. The renowned Ventrar route, which follows, entails crossing a string of gullies with stretches that rate as Grade 3 due to occasional exposure. Afterwards (unless you opt for the shorter variant return that climbs back up to Bocca Tratto Spino), straightforward paths and lanes descend through flower-filled meadows to San Michele for the return ride to Malcesine. It is also possible to walk down to Malcesine (mostly on surfaced roads); follow signs carefully and allow 1hr 30min.

There are cafés and restaurants at Bocca Tratto Spino and Ristorio Prai Bar during the descent, but carry plenty of drinking water. Allow at least 30min for the *funivia* trip, to cover ticket purchase and queuing for the two stages. Check the timetable so you don't miss the last ride at walk's end (see Lago di Garda Introduction).

Despite its proximity to the lakeside and 'beach-holiday' atmosphere, **Monte Baldo** is alpine in both ambience and terrain. Walkers should wear boots (not trainers), and avoid bad weather as low cloud makes orientation a problem. Take warm clothing and wet-weather gear, even if you start out in warm conditions and brilliant sunshine.

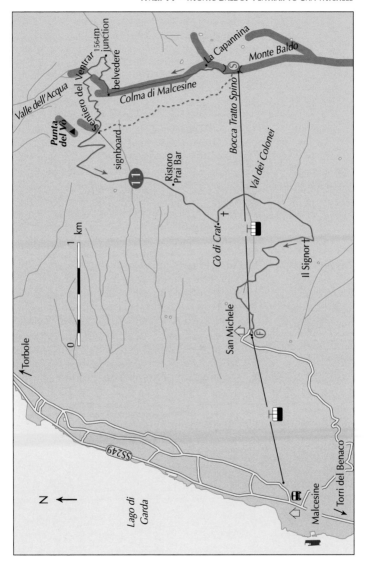

Where the cable car deposits you at the saddle **Bocca Tratto Spino** (1720m), take time to catch your breath and drink in the gorgeous vast views. The humpbacks of Monte Baldo stretch out due south, while east is the Val Brentonico. Leaving behind the cafés and restaurants, turn L (N) on the stony track for **La Capannina**, and continue along the broad grassy crest, a breathtaking walk looking north-northeast to the incline slope of Monte Altissimo. ◀ The **belvedere** extremity of the **Colma di Malcesine** (1750m, 20min) looks north to the snow-capped Adamello and Brenta groups and the spectacular top end of Lago di Garda with Riva del Garda and Torbole. A wonderful spot that is justifiably popular.

Fork R (E) on the 'Sentiero Naturalistico' down the fence line on a steep stony path, watching your step. Floral treats here come in the shape of dogroses, yellow gentians and gorgeous peonies, while in terms of fauna, marmots are guaranteed. Down at a lane and **1564m junction**, branch L for **Sentiero del Ventrar**, n.3. Not far along, you're pointed L again (W), at the head of Valle dell'Acqua. The clear path winds through woods and dwarf mountain pines, in and out of awesome gullies and natural ledges where rock columns stand sentinel.

Summertime here brings thick carpets of globeflowers, forget-me-nots, martagon lilies and bistort, while the air is thick with twittering skylarks and soaring eagles.

The amazing views from the belvedere

Several long lengths of hand cable are encountered, as are brilliant viewing points down to the lake. In 30min you're out of the gullies close to Punta del Vò, and at a signboard marking the end of Sentiero del Ventrar (1560m, 50min). A wonderful picnic spot, with the vast slope beneath the Cime del Ventrar affording magnificent views to the lake and across to Limone, not to mention Malcesine far below. The variant return route strikes out from here, as follows.

Return to Bocca Tratto Spino (45min)

From the signboard (1560m) it is feasible to take the clear if narrow path n.16 marked in red/white that cuts SSE in constant ascent across the flowered slope, concluding at **Bocca Tratto Spino** and the upper cable-car station.

From the **signboard** follow the path downhill marked for 'Prai ristorante/bar'. Amidst spreads of white St Bruno's lilies, it proceeds NW flanked by walls dating back to World War I. A sharp bend L marks the start of wide curves through lush meadows bright with orange lilies. Still as n.3 the way becomes a lane S past chalets and huts in farmland. After **Ristoro Prai Bar** (1300m, 30min) continue in gentle descent to a panoramic bench set on the outcrop **Cò di Crat** (1214m).

Now the lane takes a plunge S past a shrine down Val dei Colonei under the *funivia* cables and into woodland. Further on is the path junction **Il Signor** (981m, 30min) where you keep R through a curious chapel whose roof covers the track. It contains plaques in memory of accident victims from the 1870s. An old paved track (n.2/3) NE heads downhill through conifers and past benches, the steeper stretches of the lane cemented over. After wide curves and passing under the cables again, you reach rural landscape with farms then the tiny settlement of **San Michele** (561m, 50min) and the middle station of the cable car, not to mention the inviting café terrace of nearby Locanda Monte Baldo. This is the conclusion of the walk.

WALK 12
Monte Baldo: Cima delle Pozzette

Start/Finish	Bocca Tratto Spino cable-car station
Distance	10.5km (6.5 miles)
Ascent/Descent	415m/415m
Difficulty	Grade 2
Walking time	2hr 45min (+ 30min for cable car)
Access	Malcesine is reached by ferry or ATV bus from Torbole or Torri del Benaco and Verona; the *funivia* (cable car) station is very close to the town centre

An exquisitely panoramic walk along the crest of Monte Baldo to the Cima delle Pozzette above the northeastern shores of Lago di Garda. The day begins with the thrilling two-stage cable-car ride from Malcesine (allow at least an extra 30min for queuing, ticket purchase and the change of cabin en route).

The initial section follows the broad north–south crest of Monte Baldo, which gradually narrows as it ascends in a series of humps. This popular route is well within the capability of average walkers, though it is inadvisable prior to mid-June in case of late-lying snow which can cover waymarking and may be dangerous. Pick a clear day and start out as early as possible to beat cloud cover.

In calm conditions experienced walkers who do not suffer from vertigo can extend the route to 2218m **Cima Valdritta**, the loftiest point on Monte Baldo. This entails a further 3hr on a constantly exposed ridge (Grade 3+ – see below).

From the cable-car station at **Bocca Tratto Spino** (1720m), turn R (S) and set out downhill past the **Baita dei Forti** restaurant. At the dirt track and ski lift go straight up the shoulder on the other side, on well-trodden path n.651. It climbs steadily through grass and alpenrose shrubs, though your attention will undoubtedly be drawn to the wonderful views of the lake and Monte Baldo peaks ahead. You reach a **chair lift** (1833m, 30min) that comes from Pra Alpesina on the eastern flanks. From here are great bird's-eye views of Malcesine on its promontory.

The path soon enters the Lastoni Selva Pezzi **Nature Reserve** where walkers must not leave the red/white marked path for any reason. You traverse meadows bright with scented daphne and primulas, heading steadily uphill with exciting glimpses of the Adige river valley to the east and the Pasubio massif beyond. The path moves gradually SSW to become rockier, narrowing a little to pass through corridors of springy dwarf mountain pine, requiring the

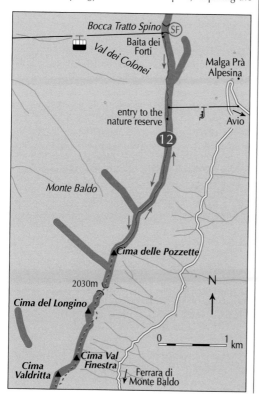

occasional hands-on scramble. With an all-round out-look you gain the wooden cross on **Cima delle Pozzette** (2132m, 1hr), a magnificent spot that feels like the top of the world! The dramatic cliffs around Campione on the western shores of Lago di Garda can be admired, along with the sweep of the lower lake and the plain.

Extension to Cima Valdritta (3hr return)

Weather and energy permitting, continue SSW in steep descent at first along the rapidly narrowing ridge route to a 2030m **saddle**. Veering L the path detours below **Cima del Longino**. Fixed cables then guide walkers along to 2086m **Cima Val Finestra** prior to Forcella di Valdritta (2107m). Here a tricky scramble detours to the peak of **Cima Valdritta** (2218m, 1hr 30min). This is the highest point on Monte Baldo. Afterwards, taking great care, retrace your steps to **Cima delle Pozzette** (1hr 30min).

The entrance to the Nature Reserve

In terms of panoramas, the return leg to **Bocca Tratto Spino** (1720m, 1hr 15min) is almost better than the outward climb as you are now looking north towards the Alps.

WALK 13

Monte Baldo: Eremo SS Benigno e Caro

Start	San Michele middle cable-car station
Finish	Hotel Cassone bus stop
Distance	12.5km (7.8 miles)
Ascent/Descent	570m/1050m
Difficulty	Grade 1–2
Walking time	3hr 30min (+ 20min for cable car)
Access	The *funivia* (cable-car) station at Malcesine is close to the town centre. Alight at the middle station (San Michele). From Cassone an ATV bus or the hourly summer shuttle Tourist Bus returns to Malcesine.

A long but straightforward route along the midriff of Monte Baldo high above the town of Malcesine. Very few other walkers will be encountered as you wander through farmland and dense woodland to an atmospheric chapel on the site of a remote and ancient *eremo* (hermitage) at the foot of towering cliffs in a dramatic valley. The ensuing descent to the lakeside takes steep pathways and lanes to the flourishing olive groves of Cassone, from where it's but a short bus ride back to Malcesine.

No cafés or shops are encountered en route so take lunch and drinking water.

From **San Michele** (561m) walk uphill to the signpost for path n.13 and continue up past a house to a clear junction. Ignore the fork L for Monte Baldo and go R (S) on the forestry track (n.13) to reach the **Chiesa di San Michele**. Keep following the red/white waymarks down the stony path SSW between meadows and small farms in common with a mountain bike (MTB) trail for a while. Steep at times, it drops to a house (**Le Vignole**) and a concreted road.

Where this veers R, keep straight ahead above farming settlements and olive groves in Val di Monte. Flanking

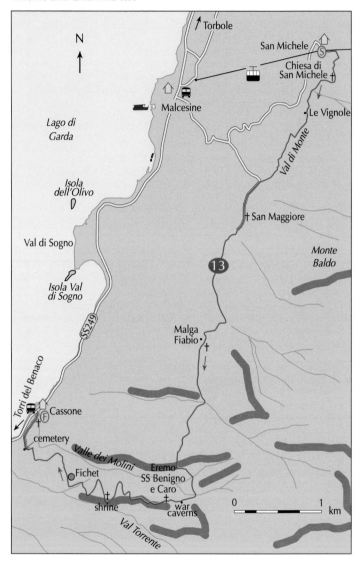

a fence around a State Forest (*Foresta Demaniale*), an undulating forestry lane leads past new housing and through to a surfaced road. You've now joined n.1; fork L uphill on the tarmac past fields and farms at the base of the awesome inclined forested slabs of Monte Baldo. A handy landmark soon reached is the roadside shrine of **San Maggiore** (435m, 45min). A gravel lane then leads past a quiet group of houses, including an *Agriturismo* with lovely lake views.

A lane leads steadily uphill through beech woodland for a long stretch, finally veering R and up to power lines and a pylon on a broad shoulder hosting the abandoned farm of **Malga Fiabio** (721m, 45min). Bright with orange lilies, the clearing gives wonderful views over the lake and up to the jagged towers and cliffs of Monte Baldo virtually overhead. Continuing S the way passes a shrine and proceeds uphill into wood. Not far along is a modest rock 'gateway'; thereafter the altitude oscillates around the 800m mark for a while. An abrupt descent takes a cutting through pink limestone with a view to magnificent cliffs opposite on the shovel-shaped Pala di San

San Maggiore shrine

Zeno, its majesty becoming clearer as you traverse Valle dei Molini.

Curving R (W), it's not far past **wartime rock caverns** to the **Eremo SS Benigno e Caro** (830m, 45min). The charming spot is alive with birdsong. The reconstructed church is locked, though the original cell where the hermits dwelt is always open. The building looks up to a clutch of peaks and rock points on the highest part of Monte Baldo, impossible slopes cloaked in trees.

> The cell was the long-term dwelling of two 8th-century hermits **Benigno and Caro**, renowned for their wisdom. King Pepin, son of the Holy Roman Emperor Charlemagne, came often to seek their counsel. ('SS' stands for *santi*, saints.)

Only metres along the path from the building a bench affords a lovely outlook over the lake. Soon, past trenches and crumbling walls dating back to World War I, an old paved mule track (n.1) heads downhill on a shoulder outcrop between two deep dramatic valleys that plunge directly from the summits of the Monte Baldo range. Near a **shrine** (542m) is an excellent viewpoint back up Val Torrente to Monte Telegrafo.

Continue down to the hamlet of **Fichet** (304m) where a concreted lane leads through extensive olive groves, the glittering lake visible between the trees. Down at a **cemetery** opposite playing fields, turn R via a church to the main lakeside road at **Cassone** (80m, 1hr 15min). Immediately R is the bus stop near Hotel Cassone where the mountain stream from Valle dei Molini flows towards the lake.

Mountain stream as it reaches the lake

WALK 14
Monte Baldo: Rifugio Telegrafo Circuit

Start	Rifugio Fiori di Baldo
Finish	Malga Prada
Distance	13km (8 miles)
Ascent/Descent	690m/950m
Difficulty	Grade 2–3
Walking time	4hr (+ 1hr for lifts)
Access	Prada Alta (1000m) – where the first lift starts – can be reached by summer Walk&Bike bus (ATV) from Verona via San Zeno di Montagna (not daily). Cars can park at Prada Alta.

A wonderful day out on the southern slopes of Monte Baldo. The day's fun begins with a ride in a *cabinovia* as far as Malga Prada, also known as Rifugio Mondini. It runs from mid-June to early October, as does the linked system, a new two-seater chair lift to friendly café-restaurant Rifugio Fiori del Baldo, giving easy access for day walkers to the flower-covered slopes and high ridges of Monte Baldo. The handy lifts have been completely renewed.

This circuit (initially Grade 1) follows old wartime trails with stunning views as far as hospitable Rifugio Telegrafo. Afterwards steeper (and quieter) Grade 2 paths are followed. Clear weather is essential for both views and orientation, but low cloud and mist are common, so be warned – such conditions can make it hard to find the paths, especially on the return stretch.

From the chair lift at **Rifugio Fiori del Baldo** (1815m) turn uphill (N) on the wide stony track that passes beneath **Rifugio Chierego** and a chapel.

Variant via Rifugio Chierego
A narrowish path from **Rifugio Fiori del Baldo** climbs via **Rifugio Chierego** then takes a rather exposed path n.658 that cuts below the main ridge to **Bocchetta di Coal Santo** (1983m, 30min).

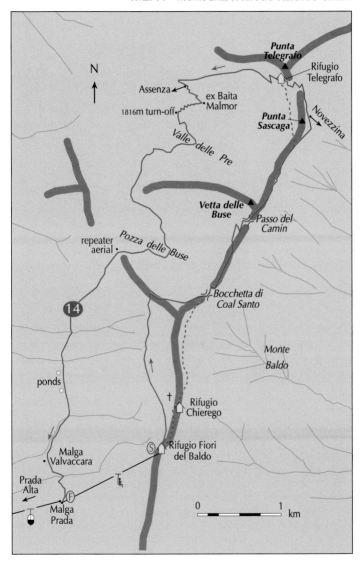

Rifugio Telegrafo

Summer walkers will take this very slowly as there are many, many wildflowers to admire and photograph, not to mention gorgeous lake views. Alpenrose shrubs take over on the higher slopes, then dwarf mountain pine as you bear R (E) over a side valley to the saddle **Bocchetta di Coal Santo** (1983m, 30min) where the variant joins up.

The way (n.658) heads NE now in gentle ascent to the rocky 'gateway' **Passo del Camin** (2126m) adjacent to Vetta delle Buse. A spectacular World War I mule track leads in and out of weird and wonderful rock pinnacles and soon flanks the magnificent cirque Valle delle Pre, home to chamois and edelweiss. Beyond nearby **Punta Sascaga** the *rifugio* building is visible. ◀ Keep to the wide track circling R past the turn-off for Novezzina, then up

Take the *scorciatoia* (shortcut) n.670 due north if you don't mind a little exposed scrambling.

for the fork L under the goods cableway over the rise to welcoming **Rifugio Telegrafo** (2142m, 1hr) beneath the eponymous mountain.

Below the building take the clear path past the chapel with red/white markings for n.654. It descends gently W, high over a cirque. After a long straight stretch, it veers L then R to a brown sign (30min) – here you leave the path headed for Assenza and instead fork L on 'Sentiero Naturalistico'. Wide zigzags lead S through dwarf mountain pine into a pasture platform once occupied by a summer farm (**ex Baita Malmor** 1884m). The path goes R for a short stretch then soon careers down a gully.

Take care not to miss the 1816m **turn-off** L (20min) – an arrow painted on the rock shows the way. Hugging a cliff base, you move into the wild neighbouring gully, the way narrow but clear. A tunnel of dwarf pines leads to a clump of fractured fallen rocks (marked by a pole for point n.8 on the Sentiero Naturalistico). Here you veer R around a white rock barrier and through a sea of conifers then up, up and steeply up to an unnamed saddle (n.7 on Sentiero Naturalistico) with dizzy views to Lago di Garda.

A misty arrival in Pozza delle Buse

The path curves L (SE) to enter the superb vast cirque **Pozza delle Buse** dominated by Vette delle Buse, so named for its sinkholes. Marmots galore! In gradual descent you leave the amphitheatre W past a huge **repeater aerial**, and Prada Alta and the lake soon come into sight below. The path is fainter now, often confused with the tracks of sheep brought up here to graze in the summer months. Continue cutting S diagonally across the grassy slopes to join a lane heading in the direction of the lifts.

After a gate, pass to the L of two ponds. Immediately after the second, go over a rise then veer abruptly R in descent touching on **Malga Valvaccara**, a stone farmhouse with a distinctive round pigeon tower. It's not far now to café-restaurant **Malga Prada** (1554m, 1hr 20min) and the lift back down to **Prada Alta** (1000m).

Rifugio Telegrafo (Tel 045 7731797 info@equipenatura.it) is open from June to late September and provides dormitory beds, meals and snacks such as their trademark *Torta sbrisolona*. Summer accommodation is also available at **Rifugio Fiori del Baldo** (Tel 045 6862477) and **Rifugio Chierego** (Tel 045 5117875 www.rifugiochierego.com).

Sheep are taken up to graze in summer

WALK 15
Monte Baldo: Costabella to Prada Alta

Start	Rifugio Fiori del Baldo
Finish	Prada Alta
Distance	9.7km (6 miles)
Descent	820m
Difficulty	Grade 1–2
Walking time	2hr 40min (+ 40min for lifts)
Access	Prada Alta (1000m) – where the first lift starts – can be reached by summer Walk&Bike bus (ATV) from Verona via San Zeno di Montagna (not daily). Cars can park at Prada Alta.

A brilliantly panoramic circuit on the gentle southern-facing slopes of the Monte Baldo massif, a riot of wildflowers in early summer. The day starts with two leisurely yet exciting lift rides (see Walk 14) as far as the gorgeously panoramic Rifugio Fiori del Baldo. A broad scenic ridge is followed in gentle descent to an imposing World War I fort, and pasture clearings and beech woodland traversed on the return leg. Chances are good of finding the brilliant vermilion wild peonies that bloom in the clearings from May to June.

Prada Alta has a café-restaurant, hotel, campsite and supermarket, and Rifugio Fiori del Baldo does drinks and meals.

Alight from the chair lift at **Rifugio Fiori del Baldo** (1815m) and give yourself a minute to take in the superb views over Lago di Garda, up to Monte Baldo and beyond vast pasture slopes east towards the Adige valley. Walk in front of the *rifugio* building and pick up the red/white marked path which moves off a tad above a lane. A delightful route, it meanders S along the grassy ridge, aptly named **Costabella**. A veritable carpet of wildflowers is traversed and enthusiasts will spot myriad orchids, lilies, edelweiss and scented alpine pinks, to mention but a few.

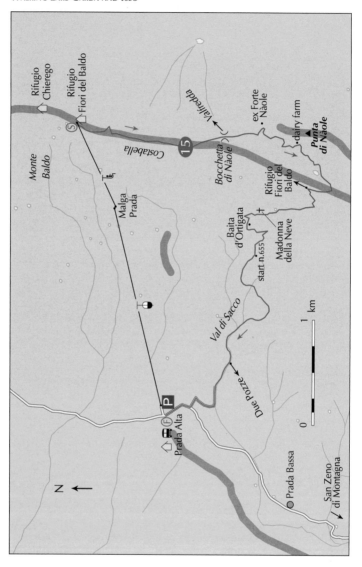

Further on is the col **Bocchetta di Nàole** (1651m, 40min) where a well-trodden path ascends from Valfredda. Here turn R but soon leave the marked path as you need to fork L through a nettle patch then a low stone wall for the gentle ascent to a path junction beneath a power line. Not far along, the path curves L to the sheltered position of the former **Forte Nàole** (1675m).

The old military lane leading from the fort

> The huge rambling structure of the **fort** has been partially restructured and its top is punctuated with antennas which do not detract from its historic interest.

Continue R along an old military lane curving past a hollow with ruined buildings, and soon it's L past a summer **dairy farm** and pond. In summer the area is thick with both pasque flowers and marmots. The lane leads SW up to the main ridge once more, and sparkling Lago di Garda comes back into sight beyond woods and pasture clearings. Close at hand are thick bushes of juniper, veritable forests of yellow gentians and wine-red columbine flowers. A short stretch in descent N leads to a

Gorgeous peonies abound in the woods

signed fork (R for Rifugio Fiori del Baldo) – go L for a couple of minutes and leave the lane to fork R on a path marked with stones and soon red/white waymarks. N.655 descends N through beech woodland where dog roses grow thick and colourful to a clearing with cows and the chapel of **Madonna della Neve** (1438m, 40min). The path continues close to a stone farmhouse with a characteristic dovecote tower, **Baita d'Ortigata** (1421m), aptly named for the nettles which flourish here. A lane leads downhill past stalls, in wide curves.

Keep your eyes peeled as 10min from the chapel at a bend you need to branch R (NW) on path **n.655**. This leads gently down pretty Val di Sacco through clearings and beech woods. Down at a stock gate and T-junction (where a sign points L for Due Pozze) go R on a lane lined with wild strawberries. This drops quickly and leaves the woods at houses. Follow the surfaced road downhill for a matter of minutes, and take the first turn-off R. In sight of the Prada Alta lift head down to the main road and go R for **Prada Alta** (1000m, 1hr 10min).

WALK 16
Torri del Benaco and Graffiti

Start/Finish	Torri del Benaco, Tourist Office
Distance	12km (7.4 miles)
Ascent/Descent	320m/320m
Difficulty	Grade 1–2
Walking time	2hr 50min
Access	ATV buses between Desenzano and Riva del Garda serve Torri del Benaco, as does the occasional passenger ferry, and the car ferry that plies the central part of Lago di Garda to Toscolano-Maderno.

This walk mostly follows lanes and stretches of tarmac, albeit quiet. The highest point, Albisano, is a charming hamlet beautifully located above the lake and promises sweeping views and a lovely lunch thanks to its cafés and restaurants.

No difficulty is involved in the walk, but extra care is needed at junctions as the signposting is a bit patchy. Superb views across Lago di Garda are enjoyed throughout. The walk starts close to the photogenic waterfront at Torri del Benaco and the Castello Scaligero museum which has several rooms featuring the prehistoric rock engravings seen on the route.

ANCIENT ROCK ENGRAVINGS

Although the graffiti or *incisioni rupestre* (rock engravings) on the thickly wooded San Vigilio promontory between Garda and Torri del Benaco are a little over-rated when compared with the magnificent display in Naquane in Valcamonica (see Lago d'Iseo Introduction), they testify to a long history of human presence on the eastern shore of Lago di Garda. It is thought that the artists were itinerant herders or hunters. Two sets of engravings discovered in 1964 are visited during this pleasant walk, both of which were scratched and tapped into a natural drawing board, rock slabs polished smooth by the passage of an ancient glacier.

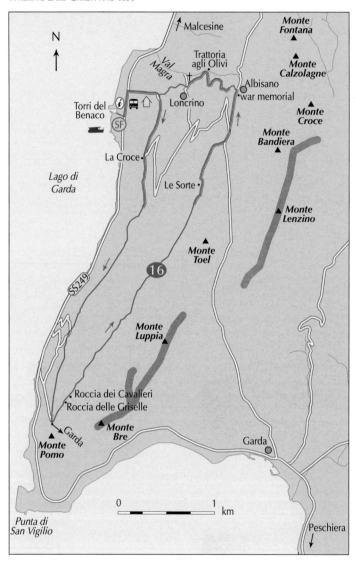

From the Tourist Office at **Torri del Benaco** (68m) walk away from the lake on pedestrian-only Via Fratelli Lavanda. At the main road turn L past the bus stop to the traffic lights. Now go R (E) on Via per Albisano, and continue past B&B Onda Garni. As the road curves R bounded by high stone walls, take the minor parallel road to its L. They soon join again to go uphill through a residential area, quickly reaching a curve at **La Croce**. Branch R here on Via Bellini, signed with red waymarks and n.2 for 'Graffiti'. The narrow road soon becomes a dirt lane coasting S through picturesque olive groves with great views down to the lake and Torri del Benaco and across the water to Salò and Toscolano-Maderno.

Further along the lane descends a little, and a short surfaced stretch passes houses before resuming its marvellous scenic stroll. At a second batch of houses, as the road veers R in descent, at an electricity substation fork L uphill on the signed path. This soon reaches a junction on Monte Pomo where it is joined by the green n.3 route from Garda. A fork L on a rocky path through woods thick with smoke bushes soon leads to the first group of rock engravings beneath Monte Bre.

Torri del Benaco and its castle stand out against the lake

The Rocca dei Cavalieri engravings

The glacially polished slab is referred to as **Roccia delle Griselle**, for the 'rope ladders' (*griselle*) on the ships depicted. A little further on is the **Roccia dei Cavalieri** with a line-up of 12 stick figures or 'knights' (*cavalieri*) (1hr 20min).

Keep uphill (NE) on the clear path lined with butchers' broom, ivy and holm oak, to where it widens to a lane. Ignore turn-offs and continue in the same direction past rural properties in gentle ascent underneath Monte Luppia. The way levels out and is surfaced as it passes through olive plantations and the hamlet of **Le Sorte** overlooking the lake and Torri del Benaco. A short stretch in descent brings you to the main road Via Volpara, where you go L.

Keep R at the next fork to nearby pretty **Albisano** (311m, 50min) for cafés (and even a bus back to Torri del Benaco). However just before you enter the actual square, at a pyramidal war memorial and large car park, cross the road to fork L down a flight of steps (sign for Torri).

Down at a lane, go L on a quiet tarmac road past more olive groves and houses. Then it's R at the next branch, down into pretty Val Magra and the **Trattoria agli Olivi** where you go L. Further on you pass an ancient shrine at **Loncrino**, and soon afterwards turn R down a delightful cobbled lane. This brings you out at the road Via per Albisano that leads down past Onda Garni to the traffic lights where you go L back to the Tourist Office at **Torri del Benaco** (68m, 40min).

LAGO D'ISEO

Lovere lakefront, with San Giovanni high above (Walk 18)

INTRODUCTION

The township of Lovere, backed by the Alps (Walk 18)

Little known to outsiders – and much less visited than its grander siblings – beautiful Lago d'Iseo is one of Italy's well-kept secrets. In 1747 Lady Mary Wortley Montagu was described it as 'a place the most beautifully romantic I ever saw in my life'. Well out of view until you actually reach its shores, it is squeezed in between the cities of Brescia and Bergamo in the region of Lombardia. Known as Sebino under ancient Roman rule, it is Italy's sixth-largest lake with a 65.3km² surface area, and boasts an attractive mountainous island, appropriately named Monteisola. The artist Christo installed his spectacular 'Floating Piers' here in

2016. Like the other lakes, Lago d'Iseo was glacially formed and is now fed by the River Oglio, which enters from the northeast through Valcamonica via a broad alluvial plain. Its northern reaches are quite dramatic and distinctly alpine in flavour as the shores are brought closer and closer together by the encroaching mountains of the Central Alps, while the south is flatter, milder and rimmed with reeds, a haven for a multitude of wildfowl. Adjoining the main town of Iseo is the territory of Franciacorta, its gentle hills planted with vineyards which produce memorable wines; not surprisingly it has been likened to a corner of Tuscany.

described, and the friendly Tourist Office (Tel 030 3748733 www.visitlakeiseo. info) can provide timetables. There are also local bus runs by Arriva/SIA. Iseo is worth a visit for its photogenic square, old streets and Romanesque churches. The settlement grew up alongside a flat expanse of shallow lagoons, an important source of peat, especially during the 1930s and 1940s. Now a Nature Reserve (www. torbiere.it), it is fitted out with walkways and marked paths for birdwatchers. The lakeside is lined with campsites, such as Camping Punta D'Oro (Tel 030 980084 www.camping-puntadoro.com).

EXPLORING THE LAKE

The main town is **Iseo**, an especially pleasant spot in the south and a perfect base for exploring the lake. It has plenty of accommodation such as Hotel Milano (Tel 030980449 www. hotelmilano.info) or B&B La Terrazza (Tel 347 6936758 www.bbiseo.it). The well-organised ferry and Trenord train services on the Brescia–Edolo line make it handy for all four walks

Rising out of the centre of the lake is delightful **Monteisola**. The main port of call is Peschiera Maraglio (Tourist Office Tel 030 9825088 www. visitmonteisola.it. Sleep at Come una volta rooms Tel 338 5357899 https:// comeunavoltamonteisola.com). All the ferries call in and there are frequent shuttles from Sulzano on the nearby eastern shore. The island even has its own bus. It is a very popular weekend destination, and the inviting lakefront restaurants do a roaring trade at lunchtime. Walk 20 climbs to the panoramic mountaintop sanctuary.

Halfway up the eastern shore of Lago d'Iseo is **Marone**, on the Trenord railway line. It is overshadowed by the Corna Trentapassi, which is profitably quarried for dolomite, processed in town; once upon a time the wool trade also brought prosperity to the area. A steep winding road climbs to Cislano. Watch out for the curious earth pyramids, the result of ongoing erosion by the mountain stream, and worth a visit. A little higher up is the alpine village of **Zone**, accessible by local bus from Marone station, with Albergo Conca Verde (Tel 030 9870946 www.concaverde.com), and the start of spectacular Walk 19.

Pisogne at the northern end of Lago d'Iseo is reachable thanks to ferries and Trenord trains. Here a side trip is in order: a short train ride along Valcamonica sees you at Capo di Ponte and the enthralling UNESCO World Heritage Naquane National Park where vast glacially polished slabs are crammed with fascinating prehistoric graffiti, bearing witness to the artistry of early man (www.parcoincisioni.capodiponte.beniculturali.it).

On the opposite shore from Pisogne and linked by ferry nestles picturesque **Lovere**, with good SAB bus services from Bergamo. Narrow alleyways and covered passages lead through an atmospheric centre punctuated with medieval towers. A worthwhile destination it also offers accommodation possibilities such as B&B Al Borgo (Tel 035 962123) in the old part of town (Tourist Office Tel 035 962178 www.visitlakeiseo.info). It is the starting point for Walk 18 to a sanctuary on Monte Cala.

Characterising the western lakeside further south are dramatic cliffs and a number of quarries. As the lake curves west towards its conclusion, the sleepy village of **Predore** stands beneath the soaring lookout of Punta Alta, the destination for Walk 17. It can be accessed by occasional ferry or SAB buses via Sarnico from Bergamo.

Not far on is **Sarnico**, where the River Oglio exits the lake to flow southwards to join the mighty River Po.

MAPS

The Kompass 1:50,000 walking map n.106 Lago d'Iseo Franciacorta can be used.

TRANSPORT

- Ferry timetables Tel 035 971483 www.navigazionelagoiseo.it
- Trenord trains Tel 02 72494949 www.trenord.it
- SAB buses Tel 800 139392 www.bergamotrasporti.it
- Arriva/SIA buses Tel 840 620001 www.arriva.it
- Zone bus www.autonoleggibonomi.it

WALK 17
Punta Alta

Start/Finish	Predore ferry wharf
Distance	10km (6.2 miles)
Ascent/Descent	850m/850m
Difficulty	Grade 2+
Walking time	4hr 30min
Access	On the southwestern shore of Lago d'Iseo, Predore can be reached easily by bus from Bergamo or ferry from places such as Iseo.

Punta Alta is a simply magnificent lookout over the entire length and breadth of Lago d'Iseo. The walk entails a constantly steep ascent from Predore, following good clearly marked paths through beautiful woodland where clearings give lovely lake views. The only slight drawbacks are encountered during the descent: a short rough section due to erosion, then a damnably steep surfaced farm road that can be tiring – but it does get you back to lake level pretty quickly!

Predore has grocery shops, cafés and restaurants. Take plenty of drinking water as there is none en route.

From the ferry wharf at **Predore** (187m), near a medieval tower, walk straight ahead to the main road. In Piazza Vittorio Veneto (bus stop), take the road to the L of the **Municipio**, signed for San Gregorio. Heading N up a V-shaped route excavated from the mountainside by the stream, it soon becomes unbelievably steep, narrowing past modest blocks of flats heaped on top of each other.

To ease the effort, branch L on Via Crona which leads in steps alongside a cascading stream that is soon bridged. Keep R for stepped Via Fossato to rejoin the tarmac at a **water trough** (*acquedotto*), where red/white path marking and numbering begin. For the time being puff up the surfaced road a further 5min to where n.734

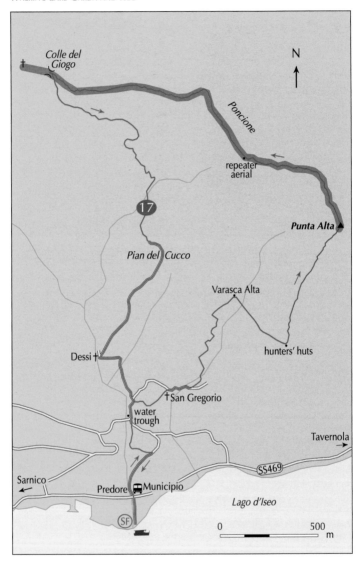

forks R through a gateway. Now you embark on the flight of 288 steps lined with white crosses that terminates at **San Gregorio**, aka Madonna della Neve (389m, 30min). Phew! Shaded by cypresses, the 17th-century church overlooks the village of Predore and across to Iseo and its lakes, as well as southwest to Sarnico.

Steep steps lead to San Gregorio

Through rural landscapes of olive groves and grazing livestock, continue the uphill crusade NE on an amazingly steep concreted lane. At a fork in the lane, make sure you branch L as per n.734, which soon levels out and becomes a stony path NNE. A stream is crossed and you enter shady woodland dominated by Turkey oak, and rife with the scratching and digging evidence of wild boars. Follow red/white waymarks carefully, at many forks, to **Varasca Alta** (604m), a rocky dried-up stream and (unreliable) spring with two rock basins. A gentle climb SE between drystone walls ensues, eventually emerging from the wood at a clearing occupied by **hunters' huts** and paraphernalia (683m, 1hr). Yet more brilliant views are on offer here.

Now fork decisively L uphill NNE. The clear path ascends steadily through light woodland, where narcissus bloom, to gain the open and spectacular top of **Punta Alta** (953m, 45min) with its picnic bench and huge compass. Monteisola lies at your feet backed by Monte Guglielmo and Corna Trentapassi to the northeast, while north is the spread of the Orobie with the Presolana, and the snowbound Alps in the distance.

Dipping into swathes of deciduous trees, path n.707 heads essentially NW. It follows the undulating line of a wide crest through the Poncione woodland, and there are glorious glimpses on both sides down to the lake. After a repeater aerial, a gentle descent sets in, emerging from the trees at more hunters' posts. Just below is the broad and vastly panoramic grassy saddle of **Colle del Giogo** (811m, 45min).

From the saddle, just before an overgrown tower and the short climb towards the modest church, keep your eyes skinned for red/white waymarking and a faint path L (SE). The way through woodland is clear while not very well trodden, and n.735 soon appears on a signpost.

Colle del Giogo

A ferry arriving at Predore

A little way along it veers R (S) down a badly eroded clay gully. For a short stretch the going gets a bit rough and messy.

The old lane soon reappears, as do rural properties and the odd house. Lined by hedgerows the way steepens and is soon surfaced. Past Pian del Cucco and meadows, it plunges to the intersection at **Dessi** (435m), a noteworthy shrine. Keep those knees braced for the near-vertical and thankfully short descent past the San Gregorio fork to the **water trough** encountered on the way up. Cut down stepped Via Fossato and return to **Predore** (187m) and the ferry wharf (1hr 30min).

WALK 18
Santuario di San Giovanni

Start/Finish	Lovere ferry wharf
Distance	6.5km (4 miles)
Ascent/Descent	450m/450m
Difficulty	Grade 1–2
Walking time	2hr 15min
Access	Lovere is served by buses from Bergamo along the western shore of the lake, and a ferry service that criss-crosses the top of Lago d'Iseo.

In the top northwestern corner of Lago d'Iseo, in the Alto Sebino district, the small town of Lovere is both hospitable and picturesque. It is understandably proud of being included on the list of 'i borghi più belli d'Italia': the most beautiful villages in Italy. Medieval towers, narrow pedestrian streets and a lively lakeside square are part of the charm. Almost directly overhead, on the prominent outcrop of Monte Cala, stands the Santuario di San Giovanni. It is easily reached by climbing from the lakeside through quiet alleyways and later woodland, with inspiring views up and down the lake en route.

From the ferry wharf and helpful Tourist Office at **Lovere** (195m) cross to the square, Piazza XIII Martiri. To the L of Pasticceria Wender take the alley Via Cavallotti to the **Polizia Municipale**. Here turn R along Via Brighenti, then L up the covered flight of steps Gradinata Ratto. At the very top, where it joins a road, fork R then take the next L on a steep street (Via Celeri) past blocks of flats, where red/white n.551 adorns a wall. Uphill a shrine is passed in memory of victims of a 1631 outbreak of the plague.

Soon afterwards is an intersection: ignore the official brown sign for Santuario San Giovanni pointing straight up the tarmac, and instead fork L on Via San Giovanni, marked red/white n.552. Quickly leaving the houses behind, you climb up to join an old paved

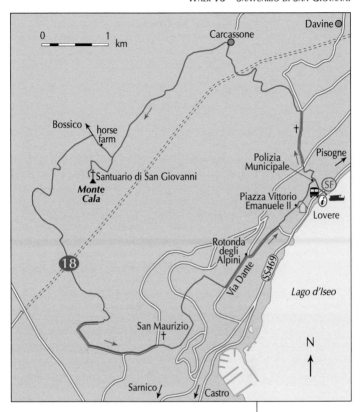

way which brings you quickly out at **Carcassone** (426m, 40min) where cool drinking water is available. Keep L on the white gravel lane W where gaps in the trees let you admire Lovere and the River Oglio flowing into the lake, the Castro promontory, and Corno Trentapassi on the opposite shore. The ascent is gentle and steady. Up at a broad saddle and turn-off, take the signed L branch for the final puff up to the church (605m, 20min).

Santuario San Giovanni was probably constructed on the site of a chapel belonging to a 12th-century fortress, of which there is no trace nowadays. Set on **Monte Cala**, it is a lovely shady spot for a picnic.

Return downhill and go L at the turn-off past a **horse and donkey farm** to another nearby junction by a house. Ignore the way for Bossico and go sharp L here on 'Sentiero Agrituristico Lago d'Iseo' (aka n.564) for Poltragno. A shady lane, it leads W past picnic benches, soon becoming steepish and knee testing as it heads downhill; watch out for loose stones. At a clearing it bears L past private property and onto a concreted lane. Still mostly in woodland it goes on to houses and a road, where you keep L along Via San Francesco.

Not far away at the large church/convent of **San Maurizio**, fork R off the road onto Via San Pietro, a pedestrian-only alley past the tiny chapel of the same name. The cobbled way winds down easily, keeping L at a junction, bringing you out in a residential area, where you go straight ahead to a T-junction. Branch R

At Santuario San Giovanni

and continue through a crossroads all the way down to the main road, Via Dante.

Piazza XIII Martiri at Lovere

Here it's L along to the Rotonda degli Alpini with a memorial in the middle of the road. Take the lower arm of Via Oprandi to enter the old part of town on Via Matteotti, curving past medieval Torre degli Alghisi to Piazza Vittorio Emanuele II. Now Via Antonio Gramsci proceeds past another tower, Torre Soca, to the **Polizia Municipale**. Here you go R down Via Cavallotti to Piazza XIII Martiri and ferry wharf of **Lovere** (195m, 1hr 15min).

WALK 19
Corna Trentapassi

Start/Finish	Zone cemetery
Distance	11km (6.8 miles)
Ascent/Descent	680m/680m
Difficulty	Grade 2–3
Walking time	3hr 30min
Access	From the railway station at Marone, a small bus climbs to Zone; stay on to the end, passing Piazza Almici with its solemn church, to the *cimitero* (cemetery). By car take the narrow winding road via the village of Cusato; park in the spacious car park near the cemetery.

An extremely rewarding circuit that visits Corna Trentapassi, a spectacular mountain-cum-lookout over Lago d'Iseo. To describe it as precipitous is an understatement, as it sits a head-spinning 1000m over the glittering waters. The mountain's name – '30 steps' – describes the limited extent of the summit area! This is not a walk for a windy day – or for anyone who suffers from vertigo.

Initially the walk follows part of the ancient Via Valeriana that once ran along the lake's eastern edge. Clear paths proceed through woodland to the final ascent on steep grassy slopes with loose stones. Take plenty of drinking water and food if you plan on a leisurely full-day outing. A smattering of shops and cafés are located in the lower part of Zone, but stock up beforehand if travelling by bus to avoid wasting time. The walk can be shortened marginally at the end by catching the bus from the park near San Antonio instead of returning to the cemetery.

From the **cemetery** at **Zone** (710m) walk uphill a short distance, then ignore the turn-off L for Albergo Conca Verde. Straight ahead (N) is an old cobbled lane signed as the Via Valeriana. With a gentle gradient at first, it enters conifer forest, soon reaching an interesting exposed rock slab incline that features the **fossilised footprints**

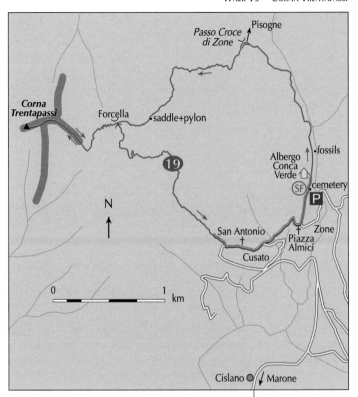

of prehistoric reptiles. Not far on is a chapel, then open fields and the junction **Passo Croce di Zone** (903m, 30min).

You leave the Via Valeriana (which descends to Pisogne), and branch L (SW) on a red/white-marked path n.205. Ups and downs and a couple of narrow stretches take you through deciduous woodland, gaps in the foliage offering exciting glimpses of the lake head against a snow-capped backdrop. Bearing L inland, it passes a **saddle with a pylon**. A short climb follows to a clutch of signposts and a bench at **Forcella** (942m, 40min), where you can look back down to the villages of Cusato and Zone in their sheltered basin at the foot of Monte Guglielmo.

N.205 quickly ascends WSW out of the trees onto stony and grassy terrain with masses of wildflowers. It traverses diagonally L to a path junction overlooking southernmost Lago d'Iseo. Fork R (NW) now over white rock; the going gets a bit steep and scrambly in places, but with ever-improving views, and a thick carpet of flowers that burst into colour in spring thanks to the strong sunshine. Traverse a flatter section under an unnamed minor peak with a cross, then veer L (W) for the final climb to spectacular **Corna Trentapassi** (1248m,

On Corna Trentapassi

50min). Once you've got your breath back, check out the line-up of peaks and ranges beyond the northern reaches of the lake, stretching from the Pennines, the Orobie and the Presolana in the northwest, to the Adamello.

The summit view takes in the top end of the lake with the River Oglio

Take the descent slowly and carefully, and watch your step on the loose stones. Return to the **Forcella** (942m, 30min), then fork R downhill on n.229. It soon becomes a broad track passing rural properties then a lovely old cobbled lane SE through woods. Houses and the road are reached at **Cusato** (689m); at a small square turn L along Via Trentapassi past the **Chiesa di San Antonio** and a park. ▶ Walk straight ahead along Via Panoramica which returns to **Piazza Almici** and a bus stop at **Zone** (680m). Fork L up the road signposted for Passo Croce di Zone to the **cemetery** (1hr).

To save returning to the cemetery, wait for the bus here.

WALK 20

Monteisola and the Santuario della Ceriola

Start/Finish	Peschiera Maraglio
Distance	7.5km (4.6 miles)
Ascent/Descent	420m/420m
Difficulty	Grade 1–2
Walking time	2hr 30min
Access	Year-round shuttle ferries link the island with Sulzano on the eastern shore of Lago d'Iseo; there are regular scheduled services from Iseo and other lake ports.

The attractive wooded island of Monteisola in the southeastern corner of Lago d'Iseo consists essentially of a mountain, as the name 'mountain island' suggests. A visit – and this walk – makes a lovely day outing. The locals boast that while this is nowhere near the largest lake island in Europe, at a mere 4.5km², it does hold the record for the highest elevation – 600m. The nine villages dotted around the shore are home to a thriving community of 1800 souls who earn a crust as builders of traditional fishing nets and renowned *Naèt* motor boats, not to mention as fishermen of freshwater sardines.

The island is justifiably popular as it acts as a weekend refuge from the hustle and bustle of town life; it has very few four-wheeled vehicles, and the inhabitants get around by bicycle or scooter. The orange minibus can always be taken. At Peschiera there are cafés and restaurants, as well as grocery shops.

From the ferry wharf at **Peschiera Maraglio** (205m), turn R (N) along the lakefront where fishing boats both old and new are tied up outside houses and laid-back cafés. As you reach the bakery Forneria Ziliani, branch L alongside the ochre Comune building and Tourist Office to a covered passageway. Here is the first of the signs for Santuario della Ceriola.

This way curves L at first to the start of steps through the old part of the village and up to the road. Straight

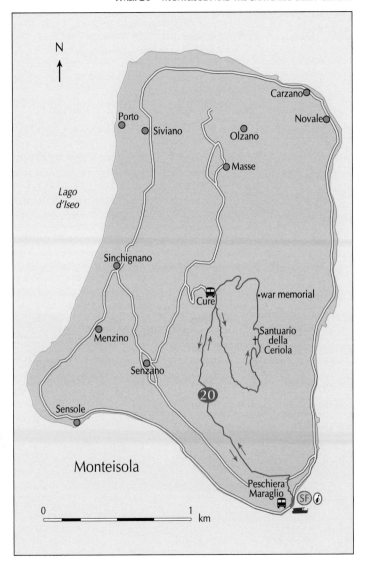

across is the signed start of the path. Lined with stone walls, this winds and climbs W through olive groves then light woodland alive with birdsong. As it bears N the gradient levels out, enabling walkers to enjoy the glorious spread of the snow-capped Orobie range beyond the northern head of Lago d'Iseo.

Passing through cultivated fields you reach the first houses of the hillside village of **Cure** and a signed junction (466m, 1hr), where you fork R (SSE) gently uphill alongside meadows thick with wildflowers and tiny orchids. The sanctuary buildings are high above now, on the summit crest, still a fair climb away! A swing L into woodland leads across a broad flat saddle, then bears N. Not far on, just after the path resumes its climb and you're almost directly under the sanctuary building, leave the main path and fork R on an unmarked but clear path. This quickly gains the crest at a round of concrete, and goes sharp L up the easy rocky crest to the **Santuario della Ceriola** (600m, 30min). What a spot! As well as great views and the church, there's a snack bar and picnic area.

Well-tended fields on the way to the sanctuary

Boats line the lovely lakefront at Peschiera Maraglio

The sanctuary and much-visited **Chiesa di Madonna della Ceriola** were built on the ruins of a pagan temple. The name reputedly derives from *Quercus cerris* or Turkey oak, the wood from which its revered 12th-century statue of the Madonna was carved.

Leave the premises via the other side, through the arched portal. Go downhill and, leaving the lane as it curves left, go straight ahead down the paved stepped way lined with grey stone stations of the cross. This proceeds along a wonderfully panoramic crest, dropping to more picnic tables at a **war memorial**. Joining forces with the lane, it bears W in wide zigzags on its approach to the village of **Cure** (466m, 20min).

From here you can always return to **Peschiera** by the local bus. ▶ Otherwise retrace the outward route, not an unpleasant proposition as it gives you time to admire the views towards Iseo and the neighbouring marshy lakes as you return to **Peschiera Maraglio** (205m, 40min).

A seasonal bus connects Cure with Peschiera (early April–early October).

APPENDIX A

Route summary table

Walk no	Name	Time	Distance	Ascent/ Descent	Grade	Page
1	Valle delle Cartiere	2hr	7.3km (4.5 miles)	400m/400m	1–2	31
2	Eremo di San Valentino	3hr 45min	10km (6.2 miles)	650m/650m	2	36
3	Campione to Pregasio Loop	4hr	9.7km (6 miles)	670m/670m	2	41
4	Campione to Pieve Loop	3hr	8.3km (5.1 miles)	780m/780m	2	46
5	Limone sul Garda and the Valle del Singol	4hr 30min	10km (6.2 miles)	880m/880m	3	52
6	Monte Nodice and Pregasina	3hr 10min	8.5km (5.3 miles)	600m/600m	2–3	56
7	Strada del Ponale to Pregasina	4hr 15min	12km (7.5 miles)	470m/470m	1	61
8	The Venetian Bastione	1hr 30min	4.5km (2.8 miles)	320m/320m	1	64
9	Monte Brione	2hr 15min	7.5km (4.7 miles)	300m/300m	1–2	67
10	Torbole to Tempesta	2hr 10min	6.3km (4 miles)	270m/270m	2	70
11	Monte Baldo: Ventrar to San Michele	3hr	11.2km (7 miles)	0m/1160m	2–3	74

Walk no	Name	Time	Distance	Ascent/ Descent	Grade	Page
12	Monte Baldo: Cima delle Pozzette	2hr 45min	10.5km (6.5 miles)	415m/415m	2	78
13	Monte Baldo: Eremo SS Benigno e Caro	3hr 30min	12.5km (7.8 miles)	570m/1050m	1–2	81
14	Monte Baldo: Rifugio Telegrafo Circuit	4hr	13km (8 miles)	690m/950m	2–3	86
15	Monte Baldo: Costabella to Prada Alta	2hr 40min	9.7km (6 miles)	0m/820m	1–2	91
16	Torri del Benaco and Graffiti	2hr 50min	12km (7.4 miles)	320m/320m	1–2	95
17	Punta Alta	4hr 30min	10km (6.2 miles)	850m/850m	2+	103
18	Santuario di San Giovanni	2hr 15min	6.5km (4 miles)	450m/450m	1–2	108
19	Corna Trentapassi	3hr 30min	11km (6.8 miles)	680m/680m	2–3	112
20	Monteisola and the Santuario della Ceriola	2hr 30min	7.5km (4.6 miles)	420m/420m	1–2	116

APPENDIX B

Glossary of Italian–English terms

Italian	English
acqua (non) potabile	(un)drinkable water
affittacamere	B&B
aiuto!	help!
albergo	hotel
alimentari	grocery shop
aperto/chiuso	open/closed
aria di sosta	picnic area
attracco, imbarcadero, pontile, scalo	ferry pier, wharf, landing stage
autostazione	bus station
baita	mountain hut, often a rustic restaurant
battello	passenger ferry
bivio	junction
bocca, bocchetta	saddle, pass (lit. mouth, little mouth)
bosco	wood
caduta massi/sassi	rockfalls
calchera	lime kiln
cappella, santella	shrine, chapel
carta escursionistica	walking map
castello	castle

Italian	English
centro storico	historic town centre
chiesa	church
cima	peak
cimitero	cemetery
Comune, Municipio	Town Hall
corriere, autobus	bus
costone, cresta, crinale, dorsale	crest, ridge
croce	cross
destra/sinistra	right/left
deviazione	detour
difficile/facile	difficult/easy
eremo	hermitage
faro	lighthouse
fermata dell'autobus	bus stop
fiume	river
foce	estuary
forno	oven, furnace
frana	landslide
funicolare	funicular lift
funivia	cable car
galleria	tunnel
gradinata	flight of steps

Italian	English
guado	stream or river ford
incisione rupestre	rock engraving
inferiore/superiore	lower/upper
isola	island
lago	lake
lungolago	lakefront promenade
maneggio	horse riding
molino, mulino	mill
montagna, monte, monti	mountain or high-altitude pasture
mulattiera	old mule track
orario	timetable
orrido	ravine
panificio	bakery
passeggiata pedonale	pedestrian promenade
pasticceria	cake shop
pedoni	pedestrians
pericolo!	danger!
orrido	ravine
piazza	village or town square
pizzo, vetta	peak
ponte	bridge
previsioni del tempo	weather forecast
pronto soccorso	first aid/emergency ward
rifugio	mountain hut

Italian	English
rio, torrente	mountain stream
ristoro	refreshments, café
scalinata	flight of steps
scorciatoia	shortcut
seggiovia	chair lift
sentiero	path
soccorso alpino	mountain rescue
sorgente	spring (water)
sottopassaggio	underpass
spiaggia	beach
stazione ferroviaria	railway station
sterrata	lane, unsurfaced road
strada, via	road
supermercato	supermarket
teleferica	goods cableway
torre	tower
traghetto	car ferry
trattoria	rustic-style restaurant
vecchio, vecchia	old

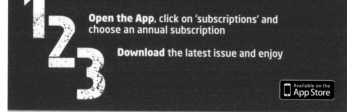

LISTING OF CICERONE GUIDES

For full information on all our guides,
books and eBooks,
visit our website:
www.cicerone.co.uk

Walking – Trekking – Mountaineering – Climbing – Cycling

Over 40 years, Cicerone have built up an outstanding collection of over 300 guides, inspiring all sorts of amazing adventures.

Every guide comes from extensive exploration and research by our expert authors, all with a passion for their subjects. They are frequently praised, endorsed and used by clubs, instructors and outdoor organisations.

All our titles can now be bought as **e-books**, **ePubs** and **Kindle** files and we also have an online magazine – **Cicerone Extra** – with features to help cyclists, climbers, walkers and trekkers choose their next adventure, at home or abroad.

Our website shows any **new information** we've had in since a book was published. Please do let us know if you find anything has changed, so that we can publish the latest details. On our **website** you'll also find great ideas and lots of detailed information about what's inside every guide and you can buy **individual routes** from many of them online.

It's easy to keep in touch with what's going on at Cicerone by getting our monthly **free e-newsletter**, which is full of offers, competitions, up-to-date information and topical articles. You can subscribe on our home page and also follow us on Facebook and **Twitter** or dip into our **blog**.

Cicerone – the very best guides for exploring the world.

CICERONE

Juniper House, Murley Moss, Oxenholme Road, Kendal, Cumbria LA9 7RL
Tel: 015395 62069 info@cicerone.co.uk
www.cicerone.co.uk